the EMOTIONAL LOAD

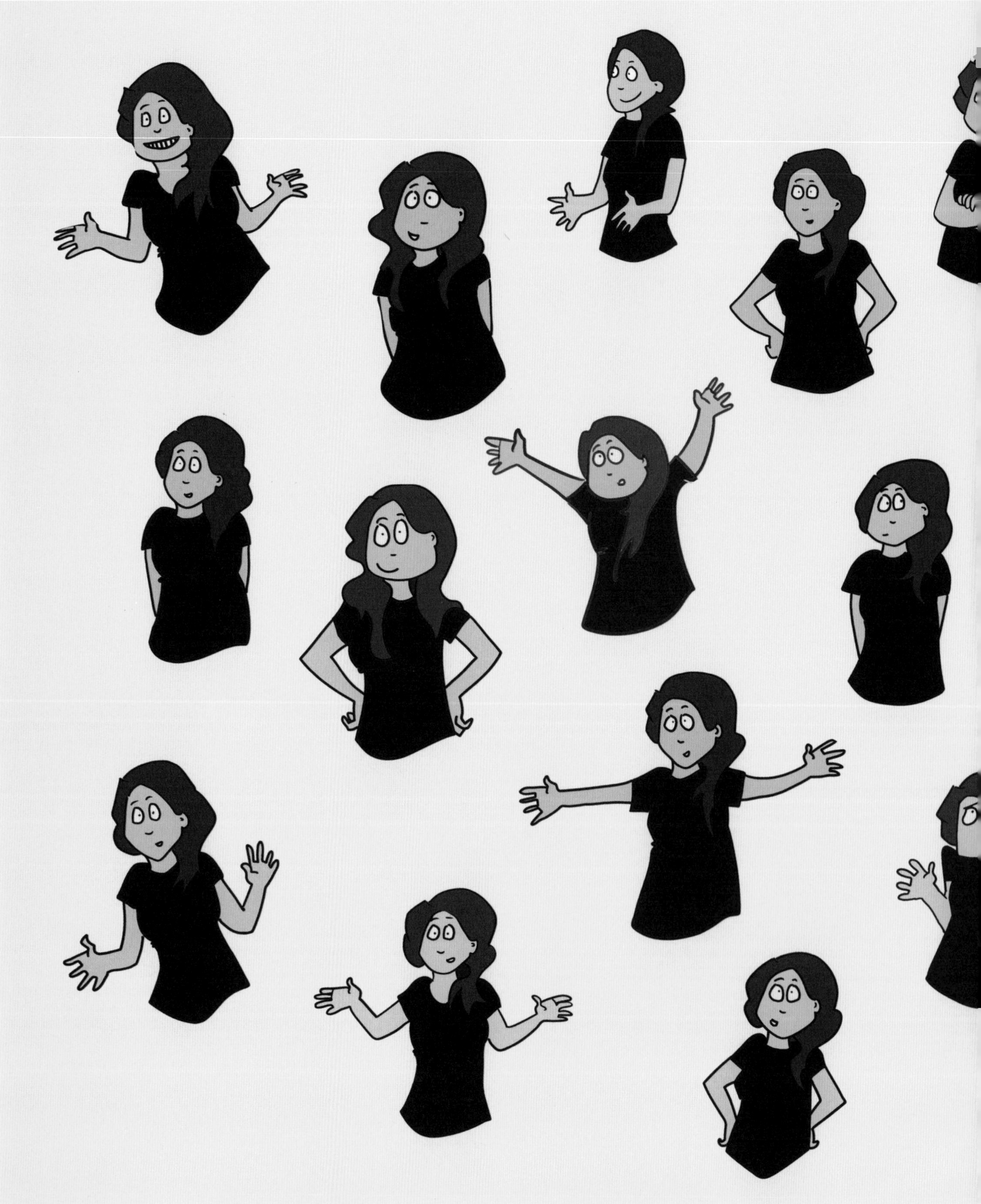

the EMOTIONAL LOAD

AND OTHER INVISIBLE STUFF

EMMA

TRANSLATED BY
UNA DIMITRIJEVIC

SEVEN STORIES PRESS
NEW YORK • OAKLAND • LIVERPOOL

SEVEN STORIES PRESS
140 Watts Street
New York, NY 10013
www.sevenstories.com

College professors and high school and middle school teachers may order free
examination copies of Seven Stories Press titles. To order, visit www.sevenstories.com or
send a fax on school letterhead to (212) 226-1411.

Book design by Dror Cohen

Library of Congress Cataloging-in-Publication Data

Names: Emma (Illustrator), author, illustrator. | Dimitrijevic, Una, translator.
Title: The emotional load : and other invisible stuff | Emma ; translated by Una Dimitrijevic.
Other titles: Charge emotionelle. English
Description: First English-language edition. | New York : Seven Stories Press, 2020.
Identifiers: LCCN 2020011299 (print) | LCCN 2020011300 (ebook) | ISBN 9781609809560 (trade paperback) |
ISBN 9781609809577 (ebook)
Subjects: LCSH: Feminism--Comic books, strips, etc. | Women--Social conditions--Comic books, strips, etc. | Graphic novels.
Classification: LCC HQ1155 E43613 2020 (print) | LCC HQ1155 (ebook) | DDC 305.42--dc23
LC record available at https://lccn.loc.gov/2020011299
LC ebook record available at https://lccn.loc.gov/2020011300

Printed in China.

2 4 6 8 9 7 5 3 1

TABLE of CONTENTS

THE EMOTIONAL LOAD

1

It's Not Right, But....

When I was in elementary school, I
didn't eat at the school canteen but at
a childminder's house. I would go there
at lunchtime with a few of my classmates.

Enjoy your
lunch, children!

One day, we met her brother, who had come for a visit.

Children,
say hello to
my brother.

In reality I'm
not sure she had
such an awful hair-
cut, but I didn't like
her much since she
was always gossip-
ing and forcing me
to eat my spinach.

Hello.

My classmates liked him immediately since he was constantly joking around.

Pull my finger.

And he liked "teasing" me.

Emma's my little darling, we're gonna get married one day!

He made me really uncomfortable, but I didn't dare say anything.

When we were about to leave, he leaned in toward me, his breath smelling of licorice alcohol.

On the way back, I felt pain in my stomach and had the keen sense that what happened was not **normal**.

Sorry for teasing you...

You've got a boyfriend!

You're gonna kiss and get married!

SKREEEWK

But...I was clearly the only one.

Really the only one. Because the next day ...

And that's how an adult taught us, aged eight, that it was **normal** for a man to bother girls, especially those he likes ...

... and that even by doing nothing, just by virtue of being cute, I had somewhat provoked the situation.

He thought you were so cute in your skirt!

The myth that men can't control themselves is very present in our society, so to avoid "problems," it's supposed to be up to women to be less alluring.

PREY

It's called **rape culture.**

My classmates grew up in this culture. In elementary school, some of the boys would chase after us to lift up our skirts.

Nothing wrong with that, after all, adults even sing about doing it.

In middle school, they started undoing our bras in class.

And in high school, they started touching our behinds and kissing us by surprise.

I had my first sexual experience at eighteen. My partner was domineering,

but I'd got it into my head that this was just the way things were, so I didn't really stand up for myself.

We knew that forcing someone was bad, but we'd also been told that the people who did that were strangers.

Sexual attacker recognized as such

They had to be ugly, violent, and hiding in parking lots or dark alleyways.

My boyfriend was neither a stranger, nor ugly, nor violent. He was just a regular guy with a tendency to be domineering,

who had grown up in a culture that encouraged this.

When chatting about it with my friends, I realized that most of us had had similar experiences.

I started to understand that to fight rape culture, chasing after parking lot rapists wasn't enough. We also had to talk about it with the **men in our lives:** our brothers, friends, fathers, partners...

and teach them not to search for sex by any means, but sex that was **clearly and freely consented to.**

But when I spoke about it, I always got the same reaction.

Even if the men admitted that, at some point in their lives, they had done without their partner's full consent...that wasn't the most important thing.

For the men I talked to, the most important thing was to not be put in the same category as an "attacker."

And yet, whether it's a case of making your partner feel guilty until she gives in...

...taking advantage of a friend's drunkenness...

...or using force...

...it's the same idea:

When it comes to sexuality, women's consent doesn't matter much. What matters is getting sex.

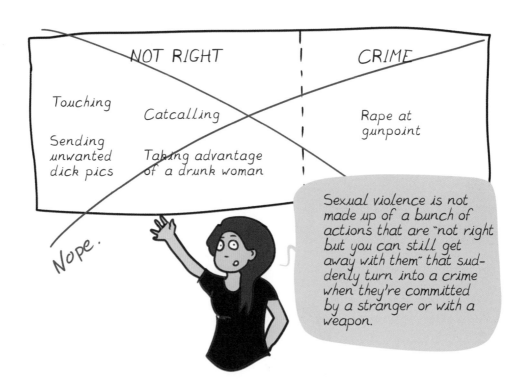

NOT RIGHT		CRIME
Touching	Catcalling	Rape at gunpoint
Sending unwanted dick pics	Taking advantage of a drunk woman	

Nope.

Sexual violence is not made up of a bunch of actions that are "not right but you can still get away with them" that suddenly turn into a crime when they're committed by a stranger or with a weapon.

SEXUAL VIOLENCE

Touching	Catcalling	Rape at gunpoint
Sending unwanted dick pics	Taking advantage of a drunk woman	

It's a **continuum**. Different degrees of abusive behavior, encouraged by rape culture, which **all ignore the need for consent**.

They're not all illegal, but they should all be eliminated!

So, do we really want

this

and this

for our children?

I don't.

So what do we do about it?

Well, for a start, we should all take a good hard look at ourselves and question our behavior when it comes to sex.

As feminists, we've long been proposing ideas to bring about this cultural change.

And move away from rape culture toward a culture of consent.

But the idea that promoting consent will ruin seduction is still deeply ingrained.

We won't be able to flirt without being sent to prison!

Men won't even dare get in an elevator alone with a woman!

And where's the sense of mystery in all of this?

So there are a lot of myths and social conditioning to be broken down.

On the portrayal of men and women in the media, which encourages this behavior.

On the difference between aggression and seduction, which is not at all blurry, contrary to what some will have you think.

And above all, in the way we educate our children.

The only condition needed to change that is to be many with the will to do it.

I'll get into this in a later comic, since there's lots to be said.

But there's already a lot of enlightening content online, and you can find some of it in the bibliography.

Here's hoping that our children will never have to say "me too."

Emma.

2

A Role to Play

But why?

You couldn't have missed it, in October 2017 millions of women rebelled against the sexual harassment and violence of which they were victims on a daily basis.

Many men were dumbfounded.
   Those I knew started to listen to our stories and our ideas about how to change things.

It's really like that all the time?

Yeah! I've been telling you that for the last ten years!

But that's not what happened everywhere.
   Pretty quickly, a kind of "resistance" emerged.
   Men, sadly encouraged by a few women, began to complain.

What's happening is horrible!

We'll no longer be able to flirt! It's the end of relations between men and women!

As a side note, it's interesting to see that the women defending this right to harassment are very wealthy, and that they're defending the men of their own social class.

Yes to harassment among **socialites**.

And as for showing solidarity with other women, that's a whole 'nother matter.

I won't waste space talking about what can possibly be going on in the heads of those who associate being harassed or attacked with not being able to find a sexual partner.

I think it really speaks for itself.

But their fear is based on a false premise: chatting someone up without harassing them is possible.
It's just a case of asking for and respecting their opinion.

If the person doesn't respond …

…then let them be!

Even if it's not very pleasant and you feel offended.

Yep! 'Cause unlike harassment, seduction is a two-player game!

And behind these gentlemen's laments is a refusal to recognize this.

They don't like that women are defending their right to turn them down—they don't like it at all!

We've got to face the fact that since our earliest years, we've been groomed to play this role.

We deck out baby girls in decorative accessories ...

...and later, in outfits that are mainly supposed to make them look pretty.

I'll get my revenge ...

You're so pretty! A real little princess!

Very early on, they get used to hearing comments about the way they look and what they're wearing.

As we grow up, it becomes impossible to ignore the lat-
est beauty trends we're expected to follow.

Everything pushes us to believe that the role of women is above
all to be desirable to men.

It's no wonder that when we defend our right to choose
if and when we want to engage in flirtation, it annoys some
people to have to respect that.

You really think we're
not even deserving of a
few words, a few minutes
of your time? We're the
ones who should be
offended, not you.

Real quote from an email sent
by a reader to the "madmoiZelle"
webzine, which responded in an
article entitled "Harassment or
Compliment"?

25

And instead of fighting harassment, the men direct their anger toward women who, according to them, aren't fulfilling the role of accepting their advances.

Because of your feminist nonsense we can't even approach you anymore!

Of course you can! As long as you listen to us if we say "no"! And if it annoys you that we're on the defensive, your anger should be directed at those who are harassing us in the first place, not at women ...

The worst thing is that the same men who see us as objects to be conquered also complain that women are too passive when it comes to seduction.

Plus, it's a real pain to always have to be the one to make the first move!

So when I hear that by fighting harassment we're going to skew relations between men and women, I want to reply that it's just the opposite!

Relations between men and women have been skewed for centuries. Skewed by our gendered education, skewed by our—legitimate—fear of being attacked. And we're fighting to change that.

Personally, I find it hard to understand how someone can seek to satisfy their own desires at the expense of another person's integrity.

But apparently, this doesn't bother everyone...

Newspaper Pretending to be left-wing

We Cant say Anything Anymore

STOP THIS CENSORSHIP

focus: The Pesky Women who won't let us flirt #MeToo

"We defend our freedom to bother you"

Emma.

3

The Story of a Guardian of the Peace

I heard Erik's story last year on a
French cultural radio station.

I immediately wanted to create a comic strip about him, so
I contacted Erik to ask him if we could meet.

We met up near the Montparnasse train station in Paris, and as always, I showed up early …

Oh, gosh, sorry, hope you weren't waiting long!

I had a drink in the meantime.

And Erik told me his story.

I grew up far from everything, in the woods.

My father gave us a strict upbringing.

Being strict meant that at six months old, he and his brothers and sisters were thrown into the water to learn to swim...

...and that to train them, their father left them hanging on an iron bar, high off the ground.

When he became physically violent, their mother
stood in the way and took the hits.

Erik described his father. Although he had brown hair and
black eyes, he was attracted to Aryan features.

A picture staged and
taken by Erik's father.

He would encourage one of his eldest sons, who had blond hair
and blue eyes, to beat up the other son with brown eyes and
dark hair, like him.

Erik is seven when his mother, although unemployed, decides to leave.

Pack your bags.

She gets a divorce and starts selling insurance door-to-door to provide for them.

They move to a working-class neighborhood of Marseille, where they spend most of their time alone.
Their mother often travels for her work.

They buy candy with the money she leaves them for food. Then they steal their food at the market.

At school, the rules are far too strict for Erik and his siblings.
They're often suspended for bad behavior.

Their mother is unaware: they forge her signature and steal the mail sent by their school from the letterbox.

During this time, they move homes a lot in Marseille, and later in Nice.

It's hard to settle down in one school.
Erik is expelled a number of times, and for good before the end of ninth grade.

He first goes to Monaco, where he lands an internship with a car mechanic.

We do the repairs. You change the oil and do the cleaning.

And you give us your tips.

But he's not treated well there, so he leaves.
With all the money in the tip jar.

He then takes a competitive exam to become
an aircraft mechanic in the army.

I came second, but the girlfriend of the guy who came first didn't want to go to Corsica.

So I got to go!

He takes part in rescue missions with a team he appreciates.

But they like to party, and over time, with too little sleep and too much alcohol, his health deteriorates. After a dizzy spell during a soccer match with his co-workers, he decides to leave.

Hey, Erik, why the snail's pace?

By this point, he weighs 123 pounds.

Noticing that Erik's taking on odd jobs to get by, his brother-in-law offers a solution.

Join me on the police force!

You'll have a real salary and decent working hours.

Erik often had run-ins with the law during his bad-boy days, and he remembers being treated with respect.

Guardian of the peace ... It's a nice profession.

I'd like to be the one protecting people.

In 1983, after getting top marks in the entrance exam, he becomes a cop. He asks to be sent to Corsica, but in the end begins working in Paris.

There, he joins the Crime Squad, led by André Le Bars, who insists on a strict code of ethics.

I forbid you to go after someone 'cause of the way they look.

And the first guy to touch a detainee is outta here!

Everything is done so that arrests are calmly executed.
    Most of their time is spent watching and waiting for the right moment to make the arrest—sometimes this takes days.

He loves
his job.

But in 1987, his request to be sent to Corsica
is accepted, and he must quit the Crime Squad.
But in Corsica things don't go along at quite
the same pace.

To taunt them, he
turns up to work in
slippers, but no one
bats an eyelid.

All right, you can
go out on patrol,
but make sure
you don't arrest
anyone.

If you should
happen to arrest a
nationalist, we'd
have a month of
violence.

Hi, guys!

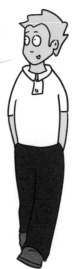

So he skips work and spends his time clearing overgrown plants to reopen an abandoned tennis court.

He finally convinces his wife to move back to Paris, where he joins Paolo's night squad.

Glad to have you.

Paolo is Italian, a black belt in jiu-jitsu, and known for his bravery.

But Erik quickly grows disillusioned.

If you wanna look efficient, it's all about the radio.

And if you're in trouble, don't mention that over the radio. Ask for back-up, but don't say you've lost control.

As soon as there's an emergency call, you respond, "We're on it!"

You turn on the flashing lights and everything, make yourself visible.

He discovers that the team's polished image is just a façade…

Guys, we've got our thirty arrests for the month.

We can take it easy, keep the radio on.

...behind which he finds unjustified and dangerous car chases...

...relentless and risky pursuits across rooftops...

...ambiguous relationships with sex workers...

...as well as violent and racist behavior.

There's some real racist behavior on the team, we can't let that slide.

Hahahahaha! If you don't like it, you're free to leave!

One night, they're out on patrol and get a radio call for a complaint about exhibitionism. The sex workers had called, knowing that the team was on duty.

Nico, that guy there, he keeps jerking off in front of us.

I'll flay him alive!

The team goes off in pursuit of the exhibitionist, without their official armbands or flashing lights. Thinking he's being chased by pimps, the man drives off in a panic.

As he speeds away, he runs over Erik.

The team picks up Erik, and after a relentless high-speed chase, they finally switch on the police lights.
    The aggressor immediately stops.

The cops all dive into the car to drag him out.

Then they throw him to the ground and start beating him.

STOP!! We'll take him to the station!

45

Back at the station, the internal affairs officer wants to debrief Erik.

I wanted to confirm your team's reports.

Huh? Absolutely not. They followed no procedure, no lights, no armbands. The suspect thought he was being chased by pimps, he panicked.

It seems the suspect ran over you deliberately, which justified the use of force during the arrest.

To be honest, I shouldn't even have been standing there.

Officers, if I note down your version of events, I'll also have to add that you were driving without lights or armbands!

They agree to change their story, but the atmosphere is increasingly tense between Erik and the rest of the team.

He decides to draft a report for his superiors, denouncing his colleagues' unethical approach.

I was rather vague, saying that I was available to give a more detailed statement.

I wanted to see what superiors I'd be dealing with.

And mostly, I wanted them to confront this kind of behavior in general, not just get rid of one team to set an example.

He's called in for a witness confrontation.

Hmm.

When he arrives, he realizes that the precinct head called in sick and was replaced by a bureau chief ...and that the three buddies seem very chilled out, already chatting away.

Only one commissioner, recently back from maternity leave, doesn't seem to be in league with them.

But the guys on the team have so few inhibitions that, without even realizing it, they admit to certain actions.

Erik is convinced that there will be consequences to this witness confrontation, until the day he reads the meeting report.

Only his reaction is not what they expected.

Erik and the sympathetic commissioner understand now that it's the precinct head who's behind the falsified report.

He's removed from Paolo's team and placed on guard duty at the presidential palace.

I may as well be a flowerpot.

He decides to demonstrate the absurdity of his outfit by showing up to shooting practice with his guard gloves on.

Don't shoot with your gloves, they'll slip! You'll kill somebody!

Yes, that's my point.

His original team, André Le Bars's Crime Squad, secretly invites him along from time to time.

But one day, following a particularly noteworthy arrest, his name is noted on the official report.

...and he finds himself back on guard duty.

During this time, he continues to file reports about his colleagues' misconduct, going higher and higher up the chain of command, but to no avail.

Until one day, when the guys from the team want to blow their own horns, and they report to the internal affairs officers that one of the prostitutes gave them intel on a robbery that was about to take place.

And the intel's good, only in reality, prostitutes never give cops intel. They're a pain in the ass more than anything else.

So internal affairs gets suspicious.

Nico is wiretapped and shadowed. Internal affairs realizes he's a pimp, living with one of the sex workers, and with hidden accounts in Switzerland.

The precinct is forced to suspend him.

The court sentences him to one year of prison without parole.

Erik takes the opportunity to demand sanctions against all of the misconduct he's witnessed.

Listen, Blondin, let's forget about all this, OK?

Tell me, where'd you like to be transferred?

I don't want a promotion.

I want the code of ethics to be applied across the board, for violence and racism in the police force to be forbidden and punished as they should be.

You want to tarnish the image of the police!

No, on the contrary, I want to protect it!

As if it were to reward him, Erik is sent to Paris' 14th district police station, without any other measures being taken.

There, he discovers the damage done by the "quota policy."

I was given a warning for "insufficient ticketing."

But I gave out 100 this month!

One evening, a sergeant takes him along on his team for a roadside stop operation. The team waits at an intersection known for its bad signaling, and soon, a confused motorist makes a wrong turn.

Vehicle registration, please.

Sorry?

Vehicle registration.

Can we please try to call the nursery first? Then we'll do the rest?

Give me the name of the nursery.

It's all right, I let them know.

Oh, thank you, I was so worried!

Erik turns to the police labor unions, but they're not interested in the quota policy or police violence. Their leaders are more concerned about their own political jockeying.

In 1995, together with about twenty colleagues, he creates the National Police Union.

For ten years, Erik didn't give out a single ticket.

One evening, in October 2003, Erik takes part in an operation known as a "78-2."

A 78-2 is a very strict affair, controlled by the public prosecutor. It's one of the institutions of the French republic.

Basically, if we think there's a lot of petty crime in a particular area, the prosecutor authorizes searches without cause of everyone in the area for a set period of time.

In theory, a 78-2 is triggered by the prosecutor, who communicates his instructions to the police chief.

But in practice, it's the police chiefs themselves who decide to lock down a neighborhood.

You're gonna do a 78-2 in Argenteuil tomorrow. I'll send over the notice.

PROSECUTOR

We're off to do a 78-2 in Argenteuil.

OK, I'll send over the notice.

That night, Erik is working with Mounir, a colleague with a reputation for being violent during searches. He has the habit of wearing fingerless gloves filled with lead weights to beat up young men on the sly.

The inspection degenerates.
Erik finally intervenes.

Later, Erik drafts an official complaint.

The Police Complaints Authority launches an investigation, but Mounir is never charged.

He was even praised for his work and transferred to a highly desirable position.

And I ended up dragged before the disciplinary board on some trumped-up charges.

Despite everything, Erik continues to denounce the violence he witnesses. His superiors are not impressed.

Blondin filed another report!

I've had it with that guy.

Mr. Blondin, I'm going to put you on leave for a few months.

So they try to get rid of him, compiling accusations against him.

Between 2001 and 2008, Erik faces six accusations and is constantly being called up before the criminal court or disciplinary committee. With no proof against him, he wins every time, but the cases drag on and he burns out.

Among his colleagues, those who support him face pressure.

Others are hostile toward him.

Some even come out with fake testimonies to help superiors get rid of him.

In 2008, Erik retires, tired and sick. Through his lawyer, he asks that the cases against him be brought to a conclusion.

So, he gives up.

The mundane story of someone who truly wanted to **defend the peace.**

Epilogue

Today, Erik lives in the Pyrenees, close to his daughter, and tops up his police department pension by looking after holiday homes.

At the end of our interview, I asked him for his opinion of the police force.

And based on all your experience, do you still think that what your superiors expect from you is that you protect people?

No, of course that's no longer the case. I reached out to every possible authority to denounce the terrible things I'd seen.

None of them did anything.

This stuff about protecting people, it's just an argument pawned off to the naive citizens that we are. What a cop is really being asked to do is serve the powers that be, that's all.

Some of them want to do it well, like me at one time. But they hit a brick wall.

We think the law's on our side, that we'll manage to improve things...but the dice are loaded. There's nothing we can do.

Personally, I don't think a "good police force" can exist. Its role will always be to quash rebellion against unjust authorities. In a fair world, where each person has equal access to resources, there'd be practically no crime. Deviant behavior would be regulated by social peer pressure, not by the police.

Hmm...Maybe we can do without the police, though I'm not so sure. In the meantime, we can at least expect the one that exists to be on its best behavior...

Emma.

4

Michelle

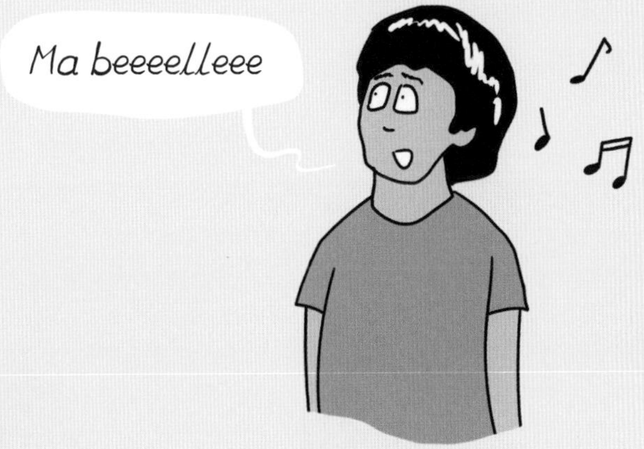
Ma beeeelleee

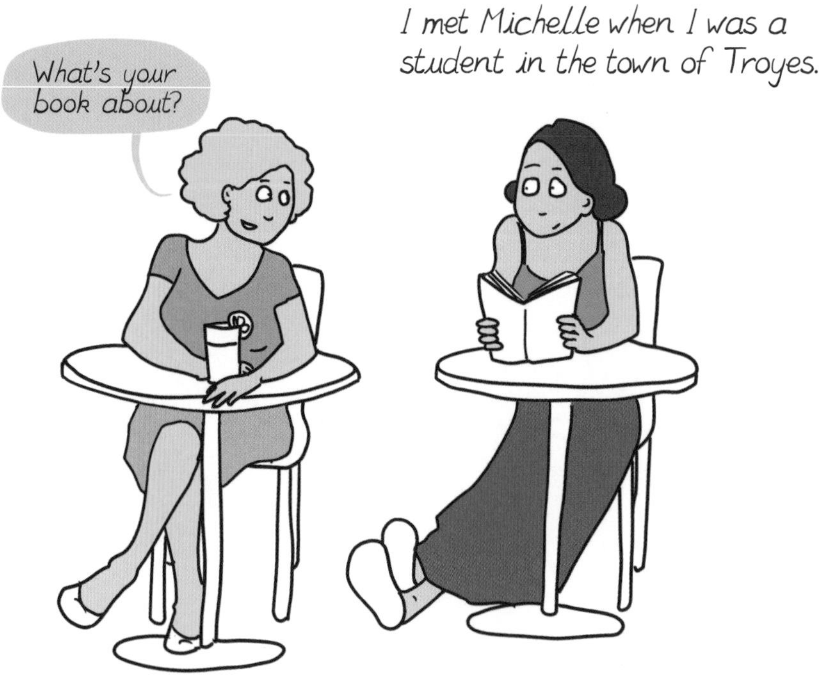
I met Michelle when I was a student in the town of Troyes.
What's your book about?

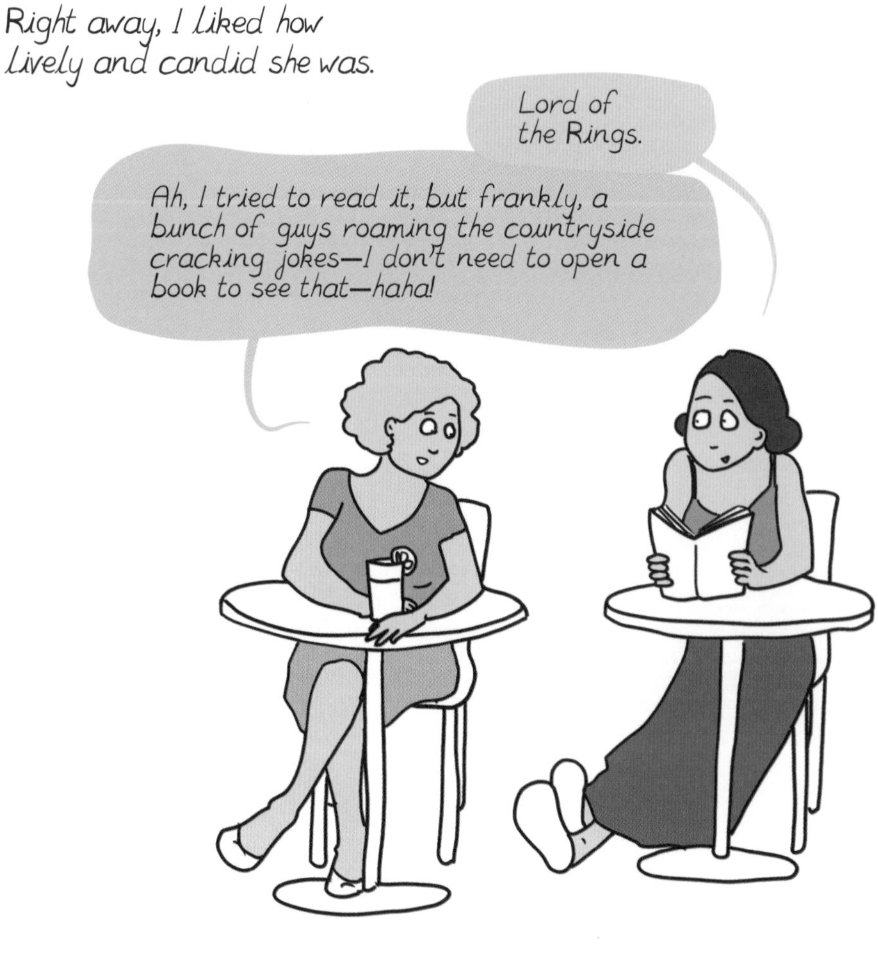
Right away, I liked how lively and candid she was.
Lord of the Rings.
Ah, I tried to read it, but frankly, a bunch of guys roaming the countryside cracking jokes—I don't need to open a book to see that—haha!

We met up often, and she'd
tell me about her past life.

I learned that she grew up in
Troyes and met her husband D.
when she was seventeen.

And at eighteen,
bam, I get preg-
nant. I wanted to
leave my parents'
house, so we got
married.

Woah,
that's young.

Michelle had three kids, and she
looked after them full-time.

D. had set up a construction business.

She helped out by doing all the admin.

And for extra income, she looked after some of the neighborhood kids along with her own.

Once her children grew up and moved out, Michelle found work as a part-time cashier in a local supermarket.

It wasn't on the books, but it helped us make ends meet!

Mrs. Germain, you forgot to weigh your vegetables again.

Despite her requests, she was never hired full-time, but she'd managed like that for the last ten years.

I was in my last year of college when D. left Michelle.

I was there for him all these years, and now his business is doing well and so he leaves with everything...you think that's normal?

At first, she was ready to do everything she could to make him stay.

I can feel him hesitating! This morning, I gave him a blow job, he's always asking for one so…

He knows you're forcing yourself and he's OK with that?

Then came resignation.

What am I gonna do alone?

With everything I did for his business…He gets it all, I'm left with nothing.

A few months later, she was done mourning her marriage.

…and finally, anger.

I did all his accounts myself for twenty years, and now he throws me away like an old sock! But you know what? Without me, he's gonna screw it up. His new girlfriend's gonna leave him, but once he regrets it, it'll be too late.

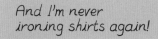

At night, it's great! I can just go to sleep.

And I'm never ironing shirts again!

I never liked sex, but with him, if he didn't get it every day, he'd start complaining.

But with her part-time job, Michelle had trouble paying the rent.

She started cleaning houses in the mornings, before going to work. But she put her back out.

And not even one year went by before her resignation returned.

I need to find someone again ... This guy from work invited me out to dinner.

I'm not really attracted to him, but he seems nice, and he's in a good position. I think I'll say yes.

In the end, Michelle moved in with P. and got herself a more stable situation.

Let's play Lingo!

But she's back to ironing shirts.

Even today, many heterosexual couples follow the same pattern as Michelle. Couples get together with the idea of supporting each other . . .

You agree to contribute to household expenses in accordance with your respective earnings.

. . . but quickly fall into a very gendered division of responsibilities.

The man works full-time outside the home, providing the main financial contribution to the household. Either for an employer, or working for himself, he undertakes what we call **productive labor.**

The woman puts her career ambitions on hold, often working part-time, to look after the home and offspring. This is what we call **reproductive labor.**

At first glance, it can seem like a fair arrangement.

Everyone does their part, only ...

...productive labor gives the right to a salary, a social status, and a pension ...

...while reproductive labor is both invisible and **free.**

With this arrangement, it's a bit like the man has a **volunteer** worker at home, looking after his house and family, in exchange for material provisions. But that money isn't hers and it **doesn't provide her with any insurance**: no sick leave, no unemployment benefits, no pension scheme.

Hello!

Hi, darling! I've just put the kids to bed.

You wanna give them a kiss and join me for dinner?

Ugh, what an awful view you've got of relationships! And what about love in all that?

Of course, there's love in every relationship. But that's got nothing to do with household chores!

It's like laying a trap out for women when you say to them: "If you don't do this work for free, if you don't sacrifice yourself for me, it means you don't love me."

And who benefits from this trap? Men do... even if they're not always aware of it. Because they can use this time to build themselves a nice nest egg.

All of that creates dependency within the couple, and it distorts the reasons why people stay together. Wouldn't it be better if each person were financially independent?

This division between productive and re-productive labor only works if the couple stays together.

But, as we know today, not all relationships last forever.

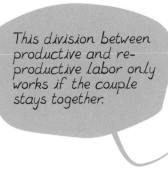

So many women who worked part-time or took parental leave find themselves penniless after a break-up.

 I stayed at home to look after everything while he was setting up his business. Then he left ... I found a part-time job, but I live on 700 euros per month.

 I studied medicine, but then I had four children, so I never practiced. I know he's seeing someone, but I keep quiet. If he leaves, I don't know how I'd manage.

 I worked some small jobs, but he was the one with the career. I'll never save up enough to have a decent retirement ... I decided to leave him, but I'll have to keep working till I drop.

According to the French Institute of Statistics, in 2010 the income of women who were separated dropped by 14.5%, while that of men rose by 3%. **And this data takes alimony into account.**

Sorry, kids, but when we move you'll be sharing a room.

WHAT???

As for pensions, women receive on average 26% less than men, **again taking alimony into account**...without which the difference is 40%.

Retirement's not bad, hey!

I'll let you know in ten years' time...

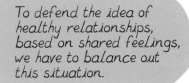

To defend the idea of healthy relationships, based on shared feelings, we have to balance out this situation.

It's not gratifying for anyone to stay in a relationship because they need to, or because they feel it's their duty.

Feminist movements have long been thinking about how we can put an end to the free labor of women.

I'll give you a quick overview of the main schools of thought and the women behind them. The texts you'll read aren't exact quotes but my own rough summaries.

Right-wing feminists, unfortunately the most prevalent in the media, consider that women can emancipate themselves through their work outside the home—without questioning the working conditions they're subjected to.

A professional life is essential for all women!

If you stop working, you're taking a considerable risk in view of the current economic situation.

Elisabeth Badinter

Sure, a job means you have your own income.

But it's not enough...

Because we've seen it with the mental load, having a job doesn't free women from the work they do at home. Either they do it **as well**, or they **delegate**: by hiring a nanny, and a cleaning lady, and by having the household shopping or even family meals delivered at home.

Yes, good evening, could you stay an hour longer tonight? I have some work to wrap up ...

They're still the ones managing those tasks.

And the work that's been delegated will be done by other people for low pay.

This solution is only transferring the exploitation of well-to-do women onto poorer individuals.

Some feminists denounce the hypocrisy of this neoliberal feminism, whose agenda often converges with far-right ideas that only immigrant men oppress women.

Poor countries provide more and more "nannies" and housemaids for rich countries.

We force these immigrant women to "integrate" into western culture, supposedly more respectful of women's rights, while getting them to do all the tasks that white women want to be rid of.

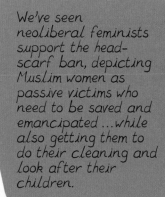

We've seen neoliberal feminists support the head-scarf ban, depicting Muslim women as passive victims who need to be saved and emancipated ...while also getting them to do their cleaning and look after their children.

Sara Farris

So, an income, yes, but under what conditions?
Paid labor doesn't help all women emancipate them-selves in the same way.

Elisabeth Badinter, successor and main stockholder of the Publicis group, the thirteenth-biggest fortune in France, with 652 million euros.

What should I do today... Have lunch on the Champs-Élysées or finish my article about how the Islamic headscarf is a symbol of female oppression?

Employed part-time on a temporary contract by a cleaning company, and earning 600 euros per month.

Then, there are anti-capitalist feminists, who take into account these class differences in their analysis of the position of women.

They're looking for solutions to reach equality when it comes to household chores, but also in other types of work.

The aim is to share the reproductive tasks, but also the means of production—basically, the factories—by calling into question the relationship between employers and employees.

82

In the 1970s, the "Wages for Housework" feminist movement proposed that the State should pay women for the housework they did. It was a strategic goal: emancipate women in the space they've always occupied—the home—and shake up the foundations of capitalism.

Women aren't liberated by leaving the kitchen to work on an assembly line.

We shouldn't be asking for employed work, but a salary for the work we already do: housework. We're the ones keeping everything afloat. We should be empowered rather than alienated by this.

Capitalism relies on the fact that the work we do is free. Putting a price on it will allow us to attack the very heart of this system.

Silvia Federici

For others, this proposal runs the risk of relegating us even more to this sphere.

Yes, paid labor is often brutal, alienating, and boring. But so is domestic labor! Paying women won't change the boredom they feel taking care of household chores.

Black women know what it means to be paid for housework. They spent decades doing it for other women, forced to neglect their own homes and children.

By finding work outside the home, women and men could fight capitalism together to create a socialist system. Freed from the need to be "profitable," we'll be able to automate the most arduous tasks.

Angela Davis

Fighting capitalism, yes, but on our own turf.

Right, I've been talking a lot about women, work, factories …

'Cause contrary to what I often hear, things haven't changed. Since the 1980s, the time that men spend on household chores on a daily basis has increased by … six minutes.

But at some point, we'll have to talk about … men! And why they continue to avoid housework.

Why is that? Because next to their jobs, they just don't have the time?

French statistics show that's not the case: **men who work but live on their own** find the time to do the housework.
It's when they move in with a partner that they stop.

Here you go.

When a heterosexual couple starts living together, the time the man spends doing housework is halved …

…while the woman does one extra hour per day.

84

So along with the issue of time spent working, it seems that the stereotypes, these roles into which girls and boys are projected very early on, encourage men to rely on their partners for the housework ... and the latter to accept this situation.

Our gendered education creates a **sexual division of labor**: men are fully invested in their careers, while women work for them for free. An "arrangement" that some feminists believe is encouraged by State funding.

Very early on, children are projected into a gender identity that becomes fused with their sense of self: we simply are a girl or a boy. Certain qualities are associated with these respective identities. Order and care are presented as "natural" for little girls. So it's natural to do this for free.

And tax advantages, which provide benefits for households with stay-at-home moms, encourage this sexual division of labor.

Christine Delphy

These discussions show that the issue goes far beyond housework.

Working hours, our social position, and our ethnicity are closely linked to the part we play in reproductive labor.

The system in which we live provides us with an impossible choice: take over parenting and household duties, and lose our autonomy, or invest in our careers, thereby neglecting our home or handing it over to be looked after by others for meager pay.

As a society, we can do better!

All these reproductive tasks shouldn't be piled onto stay-at-home moms, or onto others who don't always have a choice and agree to work even under poor conditions.

They should be shared collectively, among all people, regardless of gender, skin color, or professional qualifications. Everybody should take part. Of course, this means that men really have to take on their fair share, but it also means that we seriously need to consider how work is organized overall, so that everyone can make the time to do what's necessary.

As you see, we're facing a complex problem, one rooted in millennia of female oppression, prompting heated debates and deep reflection.

I'd like for the solutions to be simple and immediate, but I don't think these inequalities can be solved on a case-by-case basis, after three sessions with a shrink!

What we need is to find lasting, structural solutions, ones that will change the lives of women around the world.

One of them could be the **universal basic income**: we would no longer work to earn money, because our income would be guaranteed throughout our lives. We could then each contribute to our community according to our abilities.

But all of us need to take part if we are to find and implement these solutions.

First, by rejecting the dependence and vulnerability that result from these inequalities now.

By getting together, by talking, by sharing our stories.

Yes, just by doing this, we're being political, we're taking our lives into our own hands. We can build collectives, associations, movements, or whatever else we can think of. And then finally we might be able to start talking about equality.

Emma.

5

The Power of Love

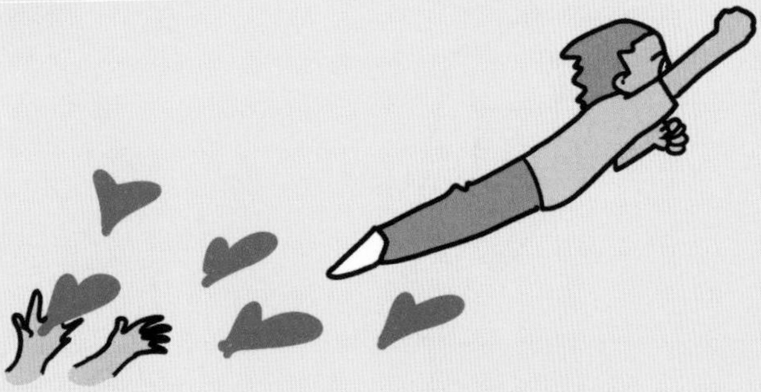

You probably remember the story of my colleague who invited me over for dinner, and had an argument with her partner.[1]

That evening, she slammed the door and left us there.

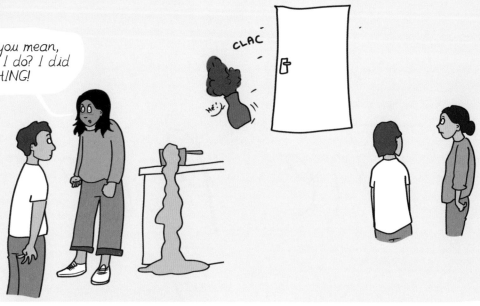

Sorry, she's super stressed at the moment. It must be 'cause of work.

'Cause of work? Right ... I'm off as well.

Right then, I didn't feel like getting involved.

1. "You Should Have Asked" in *The Mental Load*.

But the next day, we talked about it, and in the end I gave her my opinion.

He doesn't realize how much you do. Have you already tried getting home late so that he's got to look after the boys? Maybe he'd get it then.

Yeah, I tried ... I used to go dancing on Tuesdays, but when I'd get back, he'd be in such a foul mood. So I stopped.

...to the detriment of her own.

But then you're the one in a bad mood?

Yeah, but I'm all right, most of the time I manage to be nice.

I realized that on top of doing most of the work at home, she took responsibility for keeping her husband in a good mood ...

Back then, I was stunned by her reply.

But over the years, by observing and talking to friends, I became aware that many of us felt responsible for the emotional well-being of those around us.

Oh, they've got peanut butter ones! I'll get some for Remi, it'll be a nice surprise for when he gets home from work.

Including me.

Right, I think we deserve a couple of beers!

Nah, I'd better get home. I already went out last night and R. is beat, I'm gonna go help him deal with the little monster.

Even though it often encroaches upon our own emotional comfort zone.

Dear, sweetheart, you look ravishing in that dress!

Umm...Thanks, Frank.

He'll just get upset if I tell him it's inappropriate...

Arlie Russell Hochschild is a sociologist who has long studied the ways in which we modulate how we express our emotions depending on the expectations of others, especially in a professional context. She calls this **emotional labor.**

Today, many jobs involve interacting with clients. That requires emotional skills.

Employees find that they have to manipulate their own emotions, at least on the outside, to match the attitude expected of them by their employer.

The most common example is that of an air hostess, who has to stay smiling even when faced with a vile passenger or an exasperating child.

When providing a professional service, emotional labor is expected of all employees, regardless of their gender.

But we soon see that women look after the emotional well-being of others well beyond such service provider/user interactions.

I brought a yucca to decorate the office!

I baked you all a cake!

Who wants to pitch in for Frank's leaving gift?

And it's not just at the office.

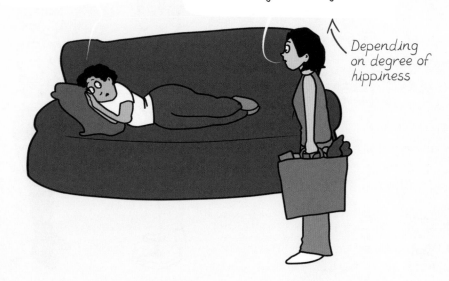

I'm siiiick! I'm all hot and my throat itches.

Oh... I'll call the doctor / bring you a grog / a herbal tea / belladonna / organic cranberry and clay extract.

Depending on degree of hippiness

Because by looking after our partner's health ...

...when he doesn't bother ...

...by dealing with family relationships, even when they're not our own ...

...by anticipating every little need, even before it's expressed ...

...we slowly become their mothers and nurses, rather than their partners.

I often hear men complain about their partner's lack of libido. But that seems normal when a relationship between equals morphs into one between a mother and child.

Especially since a woman's emotional labor not only follows her home from work but creeps into the bedroom.

Because sex within heterosexual relationships is still, to this day, primarily centered around the man's pleasure and orgasm.

Traditionally, sex stops when the latter is reached, regardless of his partner's satisfaction.

According to a French Public Opinion Institute survey from 2015, 49% of French women find it difficult to climax during sex.

And the work doesn't stop there, because despite their frustration, many women take care to reassure their partner about his sexual performance...

...either by inventing an orgasm that never took place...

...or by downplaying their frustration.

BULLSHIT ALERT!

Was that good? Did I make you come?

Yes yes!

No, but don't worry, the most important thing is just to feel you inside me.

The man has to come . . . AND think he made his partner come.

According to the French Public Opinion Institute once again, 30% of French women regularly fake their orgasms.

Always being mindful of the needs of others is **emotional labor** for women, which is both constant ... and invisible.

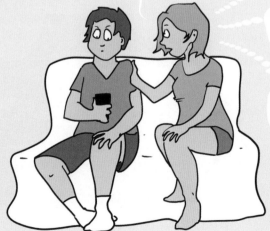

You seem down.

I shouldn't have gone out last night ...he's tired.

I need to call my mother ...

I forgot to leave something from the tooth fairy!

Because on top of the care and the time we invest, this labor also means that we're constantly deciphering the reactions and emotions of those around us in order to adjust.

Looks like he's at the end of his tether... Never mind, I'll finish it off in the oven...

Bags under eyes

Frown

Tense jaw

Under-cooked baguette

So of course, worrying about others, being empathetic, generally these are good things. Only the emotional effort put in is often one-sided.

I'm sick, my stomach hurts.

You know what'll make you feel better? Sex!

Empathy level: 0

And, like many tasks that our culture attributes to women, taking on the emotional load isn't always appreciated and recognized for what it's worth.

I remember my colleague D., who was always complaining about the messages his wife sent him when he was at work.

In reality, D.'s wife was doing more than just sending pictures of dresses—which she maybe wasn't even planning to buy.

> Well, you like it when she puts on a nice dress, don't you? And it's mainly just to interact with you that she's doing it.

> Yeah, you're right.

What she was doing above all was fostering communication in their relationship, beyond evenings watching TV and childcare logistics.

Like many other women, she was doing this work, considered futile and superficial, of oiling the machinery of social interactions—of maintaining the bonds that allow us to live together.

> Did you respond to your colleague's invitation?

> Well no, I can't make it.

> Did you get a baby-shower gift for your sister?

> Nah, but she really doesn't need anything.

What counts is not the replies to invitations or the gifts themselves, but that you thought to do it.

Anna G. Jónasdóttir is a political scientist from Iceland, specializing in research on love. Her analysis of heterosexual relations could be summarized this way:

The feeling of love is essential for a human being, it allows them to sense their own existence.

In heterosexual couples, women express their love by looking after their partner, while sacrificing their own needs.

The man feeds off this relationship to define his position in the outside world, rather than show reciprocal care toward his partner.

She calls this transfer of energy **the power of love.**

Far from being superfluous, this emotional labor is in fact what allows human beings to find the energy to take action, create, establish themselves within the public sphere.

I'd like to thank my wife, who has always supported me, even during the most difficult times ...

Man receiving some kind of scientific prize while his wife folds his socks back at home.

Being the ones who constantly provide this eats up our time and energy, which we're not investing in personal projects.

I've got an important meeting this evening, can you pick up the kids?

This project's so important to him...

OK, I'll figure something out...

In her comic book, *The Feelings of Prince Charles*, Liv Strömquist lists all the famous men who have relied on the love of women in their lives to succeed in their endeavors.

Gets his maid pregnant and leaves her to look after his sick wife.

Does all his research with his wife, then leaves her for his cousin and doesn't credit her in any of his work.

The wife who helped draft the Communist Party Manifesto but was never credited.

Karl Marx
Sniff :(

Albert Einstein

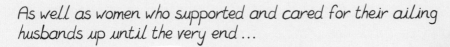

As well as women who supported and cared for their ailing husbands up until the very end...

Mary, I've got a brilliant idea! Bring me paper and ink! And a bucket to spit out my mucus!

Right away, my love.

...with the opposite being far more rare.

Ernest, I have a brilliant i...

Sorry, Mary, gotta go find someone who can support my art!

And today? Well, according to a study done in the US from 2015 to 2017 on cancer patients, sick women were abandoned by their partners in 20.8% of cases, while this was true for only 2.9% of men.

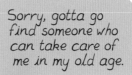

Mrs. Rogers, you're looking well today...Oh.

Sorry, gotta go find someone who can take care of me in my old age.

And yet, men would also benefit from a better division of emotional labor: they have a hard time coping without their partner's support, in and outside the home. So we find abnormally high mortality rates among widowed men compared to women, notably due to social isolation.

How does this thing even open?

Right, so since the current state of things is bad for everyone, let's change it!

So what do we do?

I can already see the "just let it go" and "no one's asking you to do all that" comments coming.

Except that even the example of widowers all by itself shows us that "all that" allows us to feel human, to create, to innovate, and even to stay alive!

And do we really want a world without empathy, one where no one cares for others or really notices those around them?

It's easy to say that it's useless to fight for change when you're benefiting from how things are.

And you don't even realize it!

But I know loads of women who dream of being indulged, receiving little signs of attention, or even just a friendly ear ... so much so that it's the real reason they pay the beautician or the hairdresser, for the little gestures of tenderness.

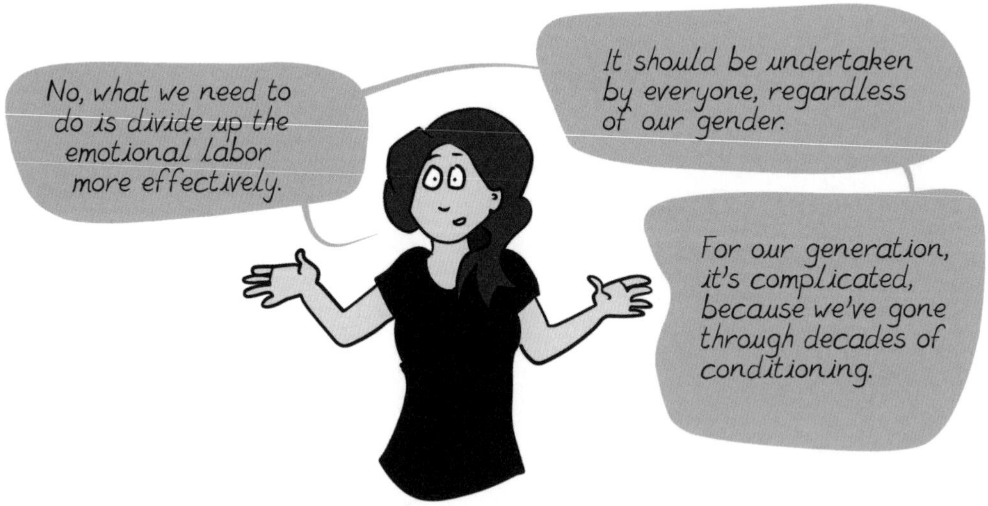
No, what we need to do is divide up the emotional labor more effectively.
It should be undertaken by everyone, regardless of our gender.
For our generation, it's complicated, because we've gone through decades of conditioning.

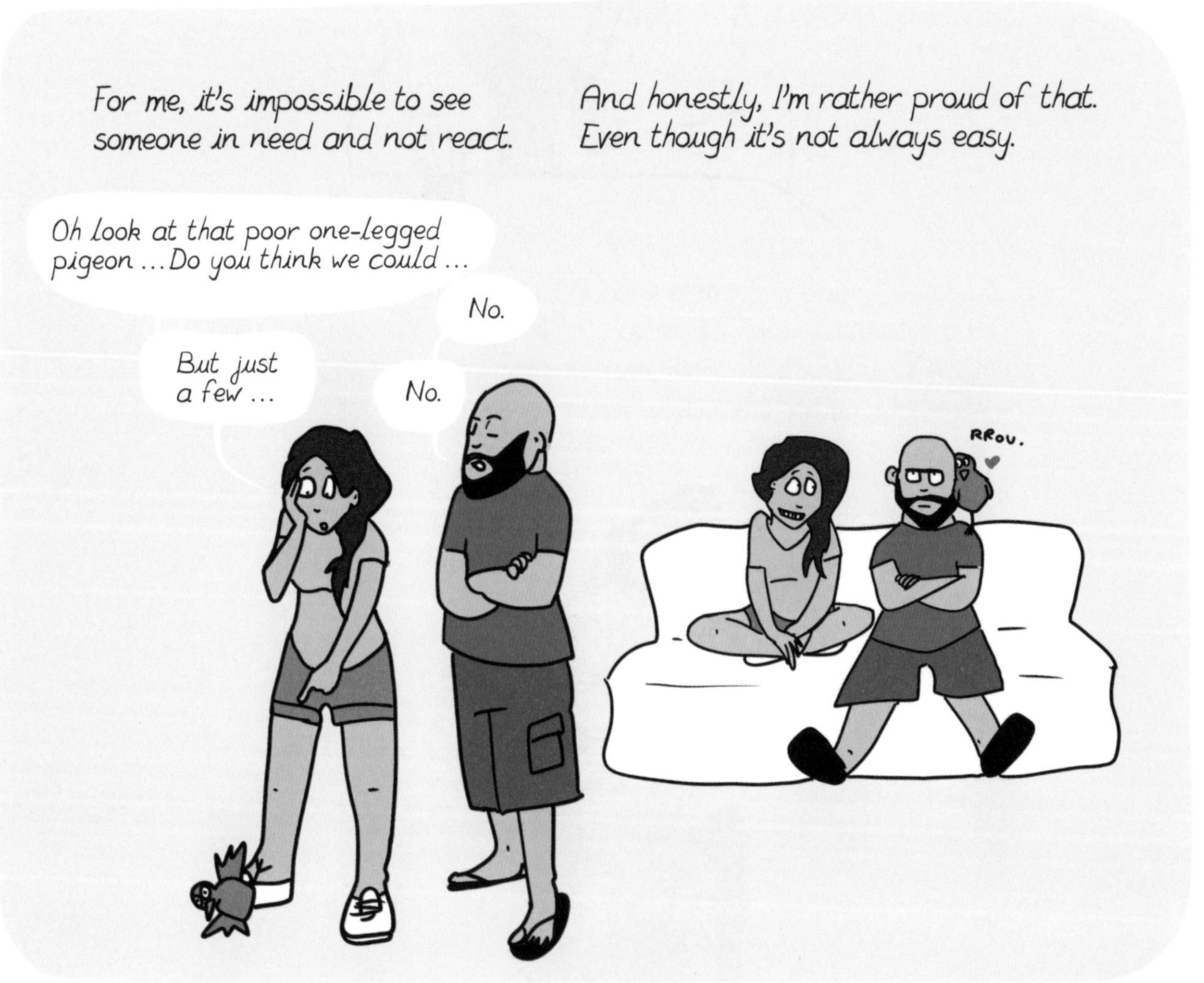
For me, it's impossible to see someone in need and not react.
Oh look at that poor one-legged pigeon ... Do you think we could ...
No.
But just a few ...
No.
And honestly, I'm rather proud of that. Even though it's not always easy.
RROU.

Being interested in others, in making them happy, giving them support when they need it ...

It's pretty great!

Of course, you shouldn't put your own needs on the back burner to do so. And for that, it needs to go both ways.

So yes, as women we also have to learn to express our needs, to speak out when something's bothering us. But that won't suffice to change things.

I personally think that men should be making the effort to get involved in this emotional sphere. By being more attentive, showing more empathy. By also being the ones who try to understand and respond to the needs of the people in their lives.

Wouldn't that make for a better society?

Emma.

6

Consequences

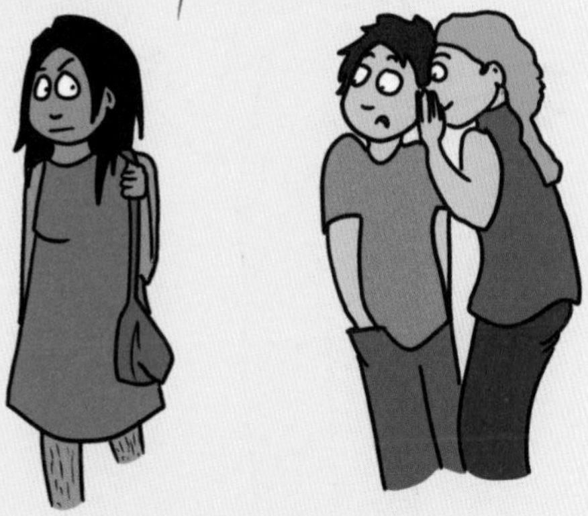

When I published my comic about the mental load,
many people asked me to also talk about men.

So, while in heterosexual couples women bear most of the mental load when it comes to household chores,

it's claimed that men have to deal with a work-related mental load.

That's true. Only ...

...so do women!

That's right! Today, most women work while **also** taking care of household tasks.

According to the French Institute of Statistics, in 2017, 67.6% of women and 75.5% of men aged between 15 and 64 made up the labor force.

That's why we talk about a "double workday."

I chose to talk about the mental load in relation to **housework** because, unlike work-related concerns, it's **specific to women**. And it highlights gender inequalities!

Another 2010 study by the French Institute of Statistics showed that women took on two-thirds of household and parenting tasks—and these figures don't take the mental load into account!

In fact, are there any activities to which women can fully devote themselves without worrying about other things at the same time?

It's not easy to come up with many!

For example, let's look at mealtimes, during which women have been conditioned since adolescence to count calories, pick through food, watch what they eat . . .

...or an action as simple as getting dressed...

...or even just walking in the street.
Many of us keep part of our brains occupied just watching out for potential harassment.

Glancing to make sure that we're not being followed, but not too obviously so we don't encourage him to follow.

And at night, it's even worse.

This doesn't feel right ...I'll take a detour through the subway.

Keys ready to defend yourself

Anti-harassment outfit (it doesn't work, but at least we're not told that "we were asking for it")

Considering that an empty subway carriage is nerve-wracking...

GULP

How to avoid being rubbed up against: bum against the folding seat or door...

...but then so is a full one!

...and handbag covering the groin.

According to a 2015 survey done by the French High Council for Gender Equality, 100% of women who use public transport have experienced sexual harassment or assault.

Thankfully, there's always sex to help us wind down!

Or not.

Not at all in fact.

Because contraception still represents a significant mental load to this day.

 *Oh no, I ran out of my pill...*

 *And I need a new prescription!*

 *The next available appointment with Dr. Thingamabob is in 2020.*

OH NON...

 *Dr. Whatshisface is not taking on any new patients at present.*

And while both partners benefit from it, it's almost exclusively handled by women.

According to the French Institute for Demographic Studies, 97% of women who want to avoid getting pregnant use a form of contraception—and over 70% of them use female contraception (pill, coil, etc.).

In any case, you get the gist:

eating what you like,

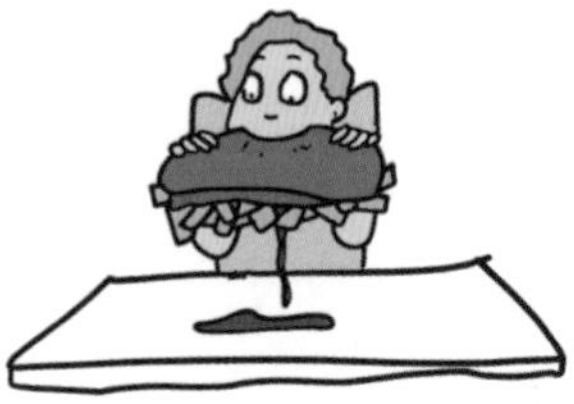

getting dressed without needing to consider the context,

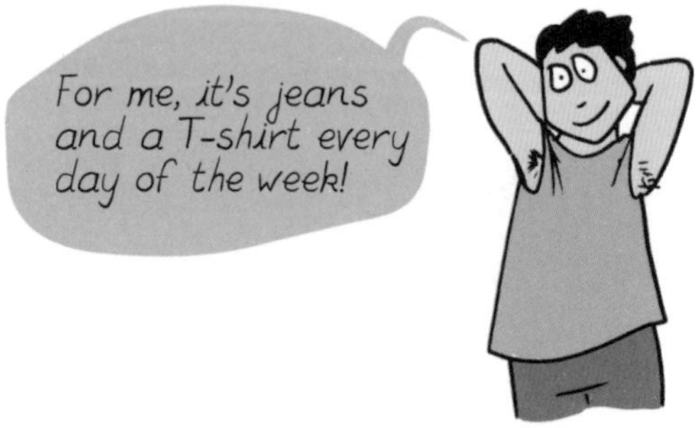
For me, it's jeans and a T-shirt every day of the week!

walking home at any hour of the night, drunk, along any available path and dressed however you choose,

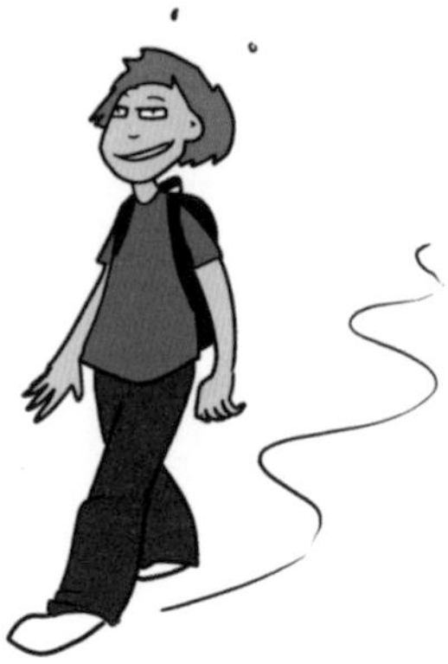

being relaxed about your sexuality ...

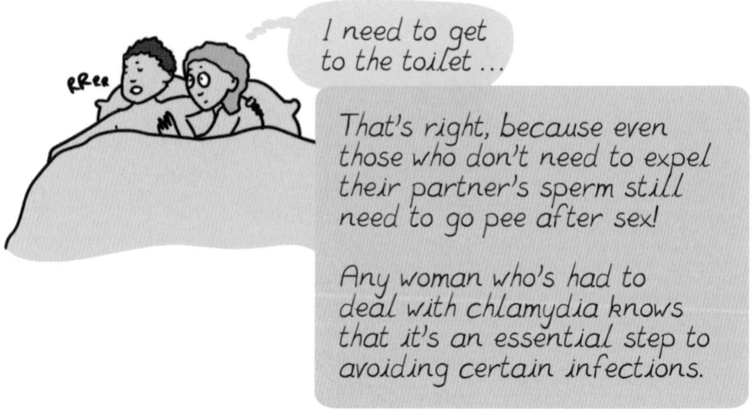
I need to get to the toilet ...
That's right, because even those who don't need to expel their partner's sperm still need to go pee after sex!
Any woman who's had to deal with chlamydia knows that it's an essential step to avoiding certain infections.

...all of these are mostly **male** privileges.

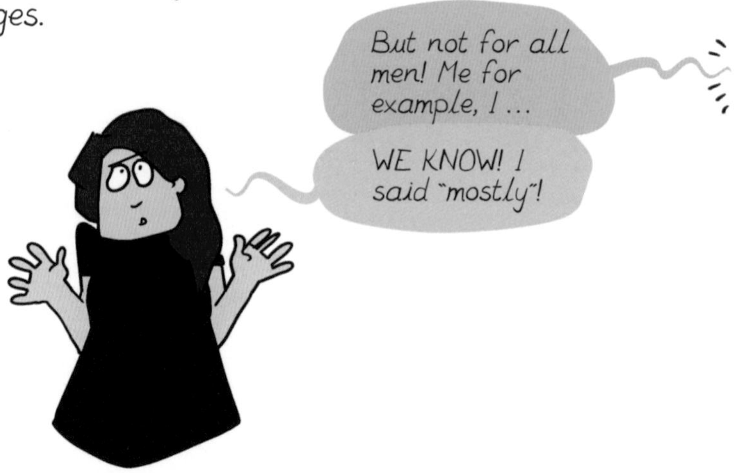
But not for all men! Me for example, I ...
WE KNOW! I said "mostly"!

For women, the moments when it's possible to be fully focused on the here-and-now are very, very rare.

And a lot of things are still expected of us. Growing up in a society in which our bodies are scrutinized from every angle represents a permanent mental load.

Because we're always worrying about potential consequences.

Ugh, enough with the victimization. No one's forcing you to pay attention to all that!

That always makes me laugh.

The guys who complain that their girlfriend spends too much time in the bathroom are the first to admit that they like her to be slim and smooth-skinned!

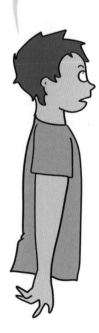

So sure, we're not doing it at gunpoint.

But we've been hounded by these expectations since we were so young ... that we've come to accept them as the norm!

They reappear the second we step in front of a mirror, whether we like it or not.

Where'd that big ass come from?

You really should straighten your hair.

And the moustache!

Getting slim in 3 days

Buy this yogurt

Get laser-smooth legs!

So some of us come up with strategies to avoid seeing ourselves,

I'll take the picture, it doesn't matter if I'm not in it.

and others manage to move beyond these expectations.

I've got better things to do than spend my time and money at the beauty salon!

But if we do manage to do it, we marginalize ourselves. We have to put up with scornful comments and stares.

And that's just when it comes to our looks...

But as for contraception, harassment in the street, the risks of sexual violence... well, we don't have much choice, they're things we simply have to worry about.

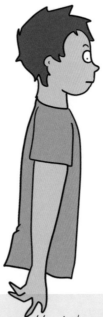

Personally, I dream of the day when men will get together to demand their right to a male contraceptive. But based on the comments I'm still hearing, that day seems far off!

So, how was your Tinder date?

Rubbish. Yet another guy who won't wear a condom because "it just doesn't feel the same..."

So, before you start saying "we've also got a mental load," it might be good to try and step into a woman's shoes for a day.

Honestly, it's astounding that despite all this, we still manage to get as much done as you at work ...

...and even more, all in the hope of reaching the same rung on the ladder!

According to the French Institute of Statistics, for an equal position and level of experience, women earn 12.8% less than men.

Sure, I agree. I'm not asking for a competition, just equality!

All right, let's not start a competition about who's suffering the most.

But every single time, all I hear is "yes, but us too." So I have to explain that it's not you too. Or in any case, **not with the same consequences.**

And often, when you say that, it's not to join our struggle but to stifle it.

It proves that you're not so bothered about the situation as it stands!

But for those who really want to take part and leave the patriarchy behind, I've got plenty of suggestions. I'd love for them to be of use to some of you!

When it comes to household and parenting tasks, you can petition for a real paternity leave, so that fathers have as much time off as mothers.

If you live as a couple, with or without children, learn to glance over each room as you step inside. Is there anything to be picked up/put away/cleaned? Doing it on your own initiative means taking on part of the mental load.

And you can also take action against everything that takes place outside the home.

For example, you can combat **street harassment**: if you see something, do something. And make sure you listen to and believe the women who tell you about their experiences.

Don't make cracks about women's looks, clothes, weight, or body hair. And this also applies to women: we should show solidarity and stop scrutinizing and criticizing each other!

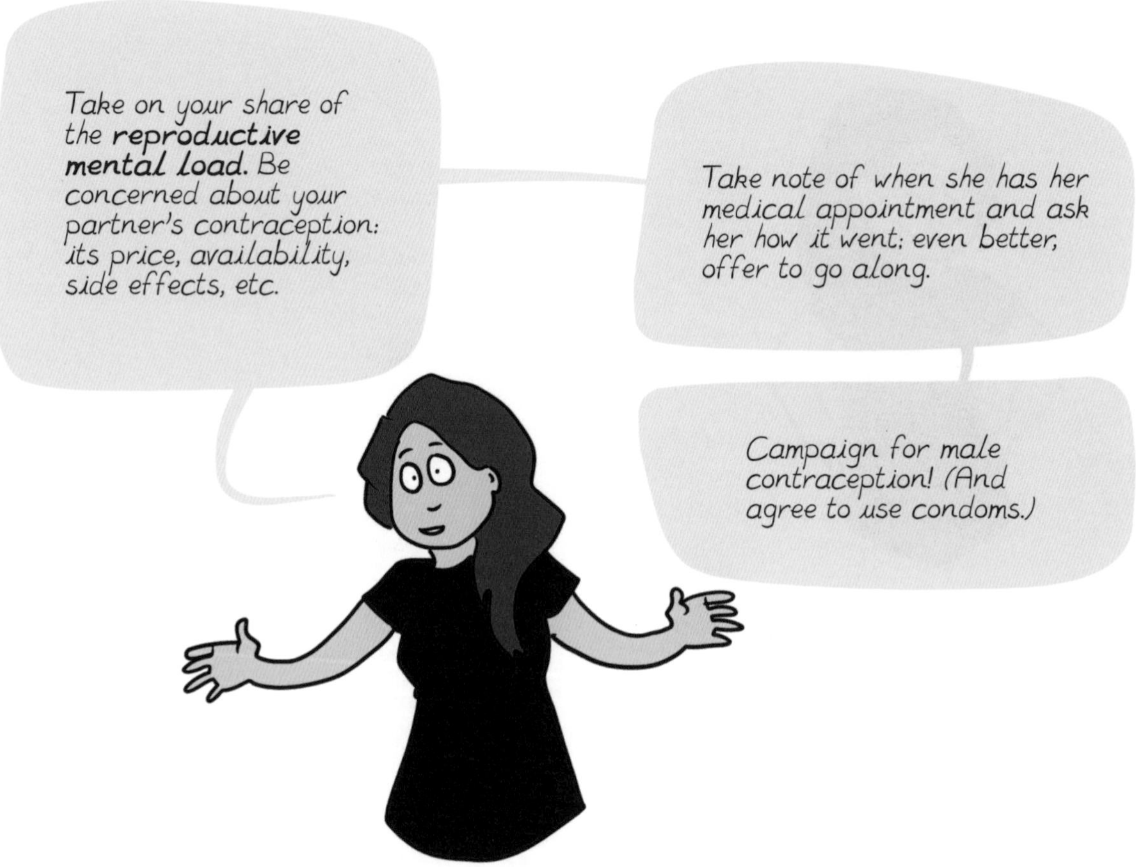
Take on your share of the **reproductive mental load.** Be concerned about your partner's contraception: its price, availability, side effects, etc.
Take note of when she has her medical appointment and ask her how it went; even better, offer to go along.
Campaign for male contraception! (And agree to use condoms.)

It's not an exhaustive list, so if it sparks your interest, I strongly encourage you to expand upon it and share your thoughts with others.

As always, to succeed we need to fight together!

Emma.

7

It's All in Your Head

Did you know that until the middle of the twentieth century, nobody was interested in the division of household chores?

It was only in the '70s that feminist movements demonstrated that this issue was a source of inequality.

Begun in Italy by feminist activists like Silvia Federici, the movement was exported to the USA in 1975. By demanding "wages for housework," feminists were saying that it should no longer be invisible and free.

Around this time, the first statistics were published, and the notion of a **double workday** came to the fore.

> Women spend almost three times longer on household chores than men.

> More and more of us also have jobs. When we get home, a second work day awaits us ...

According to the French Institute of Statistics, in 1974, women devoted five hours and thirty minutes each day to housework, compared to two hours for men. From 1970 to 1980, the rate of employment among women rose from 50% to 60%.

But talking about a double workday makes it seem like professional and domestic work **follow from one to the other.**

6 a.m.   8 a.m.   5 p.m.   10 p.m.
                                                   (or later)

That would be true, if we stopped thinking about
one when we were doing the other.
But we know that's not the case ...

6 a.m.   8 a.m.   5 p.m.   10 p.m.
                                                  (or later)

In 1984, the sociologist Monique Haicault came up with the
concept of the **household mental load** to illustrate this
overlap in daily life.

It's about showing how women
swing between two spaces: the
factory and the house ... How each
spills over into the other.

In her essay, "The Usual
Organization of a Couple's
Life," she explains how she
followed the daily lives of
women working in an elec-
tronics factory, and noted
that they were constantly
trying to synchronize commutes, parenting, household
and professional tasks in
their schedules.

The concept of **mental
load** seems like the most
adequate to describe
the superimposition that
takes place here.

Talking about the mental load helped to highlight a previously invisible element in the exploitation of women: all the **preoccupation** involved in housework, prior to its execution.

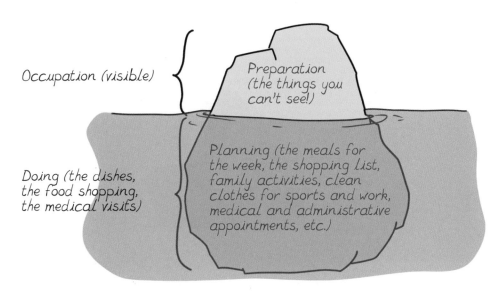

Occupation (visible)

Preparation (the things you can't see!)

Doing (the dishes, the food shopping, the medical visits)

Planning (the meals for the week, the shopping list, family activities, clean clothes for sports and work, medical and administrative appointments, etc.)

Thanks to this notion, Monique Haicault was able to show how women wear themselves out by trying to make space and time flexible,

by adapting the commute between their home and workplace,

or optimizing their schedule to use up every nugget of free time,

This job's just next to the nursery, plus there's a supermarket on the way home.

If I put the water on to boil now, do I still have time to pop in at the nursery and then throw on a load of washing before adding the pasta?

Thirty years later, as I was returning to work after the birth of my son, someone sent me an article titled "Parenting and the Mental Load."

Oh gosh, it's already 2 p.m. I'll never have time to finish this flowchart for work and stop for groceries before picking up the baby.

Huh, what's this article?

DING

Let's just say it landed exactly when I needed it to.

All of a sudden, I realized that unbeknown to me, I, a working, independent woman, had fallen into the position of household manager.

Oh.

I immediately starting discussing it with others...
and I saw that I was far from alone.

You know, when you're the one thinking about everything there is to do around the house, and the guy's just executing your instructions? Well, that means you're bearing the mental load alone.

Aaaah. Yeah, sure, just yesterday, I asked him to do the food shopping, and he said, "OK, but what should I buy? ..." I had to write him a list!

And the baby's medical appointments ... he takes him, but I'm always the one who remembers, and I have to prepare the documents and remind him what he needs to ask.

Back then, we thought that becoming aware of the issue would allow us to discuss it and balance things out. And, well, that wasn't really how it turned out for everyone.

So, did you talk about it since last time?

Yeah, it was a bit tense, but for the past week he's been doing the washing without me asking him!

As for me, he just got annoyed ... he said he already did plenty of things. I tried to explain that it wasn't about doing things, but thinking about what needed to get done. It didn't work.

And even for my friends who managed to change things, the battle was far from won.

Well, I take back what I said...it's back to like it was before with the washing. I left him to it, but this morning the kids didn't even have clean socks! They left barefoot in their sneakers...and obviously I was the one who got a talking-to at nursery.

We were stuck in a kind of "vicious circle of sharing out the mental load."

Clarification (and the feeling of being the annoying one in the couple)

I'm the one who bears all the mental load!

Oops.

Improvement

Return to square one, or nearly

I did the food shopping!

Cool!

Can you do the food shopping?

What should I get?

...Right, I'll make a list...

Admittedly, everything about our way of life encourages our partners to renounce their responsibilities.

Our parenting models

Our cultural and social environment

Agh, that's a girly game!

And the bad habits formed during maternity leave

The inequalities we suffer in private are just a reflection of our society.

A society historically designed by men...

Hey, George, I've just had a great idea! What if we said that it was in women's nature to do the boring, unpaid stuff? Then we could have it easy!

Great idea! We could put it in a book and call it sacred!

...to their advantage.

An advantage that they still benefit from today, without always being aware of it.

Ah, yes, a longer paternity leave, that'd be great, but at what cost to society? Someone needs to run the economy that whole time.

Will you be able to find work if you're at a child-rearing age? And afterward, you'll go back part-time?

You'll earn less money... have you thought about your pension?

No, I'll sacrifice myself and get back to my job.

Yes, things have evolved a bit since the Middle Ages... but we didn't create change by negotiating from home!

Feminist struggles have always been collective, bringing us together around a common cause.

1900

FRENCH WOMEN WANT THE VOTE

1970

THE RIGHT TO FREE CONTRACEPTION AND ABORTION

1980

FEMINISM MUST BE INTERNATIONAL
ALL RACES, ALL SEXUALITIES, TOGETHER!

2010

STOP RAPE AND FEMICIDE

We can achieve the important change we need

together

not each in her own corner.

Demonstrating is worth it!

In Spain, the feminist strike of March 2018 got more than five million people onto the streets.

One year later, the parental leave for the second parent was extended from five to eight weeks, and reimbursed 100%, at a cost of 226 million euros.

The aim of the law voted in June 2018 is to arrive at an equal parental leave for both parents by 2021.

We should not be given credit for this legislation proposal, it is the result of many years of struggle led by associations and women against workplace discrimination.

Pablo Iglesias, leader of the Podemos Party, which initiated Spain's legislation proposal.

Once I understood this, I decided to share what I discovered in the form of a comic strip.

Are you doing some feminism, Mom?

All alone, I could only change things in my own relationship. But together, we could coordinate to improve the situation for all of us.

And things started out rather well: the comic was very successful, and since 2017, the term "mental load" has entered the vocabulary of hundreds of thousands of women.

So I told him, there was no way I was gonna be bearing the whole mental load when it came to organizing the holidays.

Good for you!

During this time, women all around the world embraced this topic.

It was time to make some major demands that would improve not only our lives, but those of future generations.

For example, extending paternity leave, or decreasing working hours, so that everyone could be employed but work less.

But in France, we often miss the boat when it comes to major advances in women's rights.

For example, we got the right to vote in 1944, 38 years after the Finnish and 26 years after German women.

More recently, while the #MeToo movement was gaining momentum around the world, in France, we were quickly put back in our place.

We shouldn,t forbid ourselves—and this might sound shocking—a certain form of intellectual seduction, which can never be a form of violence or constraint, but which can be a form of seduction.

A comment from Prime Minister Édouard Philippe to the online French journal Mediapart, on November 22, 2017.

I don't want to get into a situation with daily accusations, where a suspicion of dominance hangs over every male-female relationship, as if it were forbidden.

Declaration by President Emmanuel Macron on the French TV channel BFMTV, on November 25, 2017.

And the next year, on March 8, when millions of women all over Europe went onto the streets, in France there were only a few hundred of us.

All this enthusiasm about the mental load never made it out the front door.

And barely one week after my comic strip came out, the media brought the discussion back to "relationships" and "communication issues."

And it didn't stop there, as "relationship problems" quickly turned into...

WomeN's Problems

See the slippery slope?

Huh? So, like, it's still my fault?

Phew! That was a close one, I almost thought I was gonna have to get my ass in gear ...ha!

So in 2018, a well-known psychology magazine published an article titled "Women's Mental Overload."

In it, they started out by retracing the feminist research on the topic,

Yeeeah!

Whaaaa?

before indulging in an individualistic and apolitical "analysis" of "women's need to control everything."

More recently, one radio station broadcast a show called "The Mental Load: Practical Solutions to Avoid Being Overwhelmed."

Present in the studio were:

Get it, lady? It's your fault 'cause you let yourself get overwhelmed!

A neurobiologist (because ... it's all in the head)

A psychiatrist (because it's all in the head)

And a journalist from a well-known psychology magazine (hmm ...)

In terms of the "solutions," no surprises there: since it's the fault of women who want to control everything, it's also up to them to resolve the problem.

...by making to-do lists and planning the time allocated to each task ...

Um, that sounds like project managing to me.

Just sayin'.

...by trying to do less ...

...and by encouraging the children to take on more responsibilities.

their partner?

Nope.

Mom, I'm hungry!

Sorry, dear, I've decided to just do less today.

RUMBLE

Today, you're gonna learn to do the clothes washing.

It's clear: the mental load has transformed from a political topic studied by sociologists into a psychological problem that can be tackled by to-do lists and meditation.

1984

The problem moved from here...

SOCIETY

2019

...to here.

And the saddest thing of all is that we sometimes shoot ourselves in the foot! For example, during a gender inequality workshop I was leading, a librarian intervened in the following manner:

Well, fine, I mean we can always play at being feminists, but we've got to admit that the real problem is women wanting to control everything!

She must have read "How to Depoliticize a Discussion in One Easy Step" before coming.

At this stage, you may be thinking we must have hit bottom. And yet … in 2018 there flourished a book that claimed to help women free themselves of the mental load … by means of a one-week therapeutic treatment.

Women are astounding in their ability to push themselves to the edge and in their utter incapacity to ask for help.

But thanks to my book, they can finally overcome this!

Similarly, in early 2019, a journalist contacted me and said this:

I'm a journalist and I looove your work!

Could you put me in touch with some women suffering from the mental load syndrome?

Word for word

So there you have it. First it was a feminist cause, then it was turned into a relationship issue and women's problem, and the mental load has finally become ... an illness!

I'm just overwhelmed, I'm constantly thinking about fifteen different things that need to get done ... I think I've caught the mental load!

Yikes! I won't get too close then ...

But I do know an acupuncturist who can help you get rid of it!

I'm acting like this is astonishing, but turning a feminist topic into a psychiatric issue is nothing new. Historically, impeding the emancipation of women was always accomplished by convincing women that they were the problem.

Women who wanted the right to vote were described as frustrated by their celibacy...

...and those who stood up to their husbands were considered shrews.

In the early twentieth century, women who denounced rapists were accused of being hysterical by the medical profession...

Hysterical women won't hesitate to invent falsehoods with the sole aim of attracting attention and rendering themselves interesting.

Paul Brouardel, head of the medical faculty of Paris, on the topic of rape accusations ("Indecent Acts," posthumous publication, 1909)

...and still today, the mocking of women who express their anger is aimed at keeping them in their place.

Aw, what's the matter, having your period?

All of that is very useful when it comes to reinforcing capitalism and the patriarchy.

It makes it easy to appear interested in our cause ...

while selling us a bunch of things ...

and without making any concrete changes to how society is organized.

In other words, it helps maintain the present order of things.

In this order, men can devote themselves fully to political, economic, and media spheres,

and women, while holding down jobs, still manage the household, silently and for free.

And it's a shame that we, as women, also help depoliticize the issue by seeking personal solutions, and by handing over our money to those who benefit from our angst.

Because we're tired, and buying a self-help book seems more accessible and more immediate than getting together and going out into the street.

Also, because we grew up immersed in a feeling of political impotence; with this idea that we belonged in the private sphere, the home; that we could help adjust to our condition, but not revolt to escape it.

While writing this story, I ran a little poll on Twitter. It was aimed at women in heterosexual couples who had tried to talk to their partners about balancing out the mental load.

In a few hours, I had over 1,000 responses.

For 18%, it changed nothing

For 6%, it changed everything

For 39%, things improved after each discussion, but then went back to square one.

For 37%, things were slowly changing (a few wrote to me to say "too slowly!")

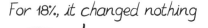

The truth is that there's no magical solution to this inequality. No therapy sessions or lists of suggestions will significantly improve the situation.

It's a structural problem, rooted in multiple generations of patriarchal conditioning, which can only be undone over time, and by fighting for it!

Women's strikes are regularly organized all around the world. It's an opportunity to make ourselves heard.

And when it comes to putting up a fight, I've got a suggestion.

It's also a chance to get together in a political context, to leave the private sphere, prepare our demonstration and help launch discussions. To emerge from our isolation, forge bonds, and build an unstoppable political force.

Together, we can lay the groundwork for the next feminist revolution!

8

Sunday Evenings

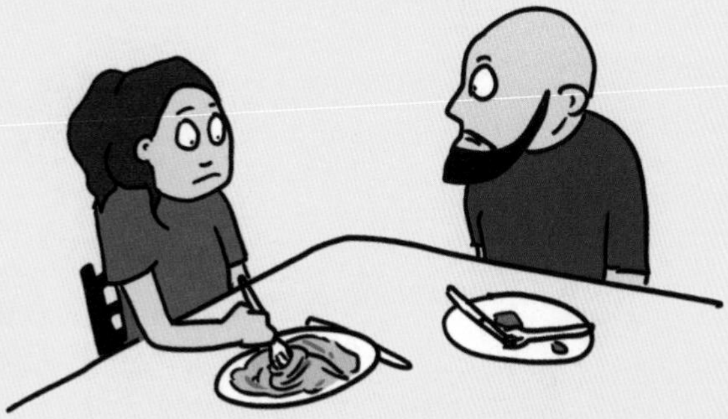

Back in the 2000s, when I was a student, I worked during the summer holidays.
My first job was waitressing.

All right, Pansy, get a move on!

He called all the waitresses "Pansy"

And you forgot to add table 13's bottle to their bill, that's coming off your pay.

My boss and the clients would shout at me so often that half the time I'd go home in tears.

The next year, I was hired as a "service girl" in a retirement home. I had to serve breakfast, give out medication, change the beds, and clean the rooms before noon.

Please, dear, I'd like to go to the bathroom...

I just need to pop in and see the gentleman in room 12 and I'll be right back!

There, I was going home in tears almost every day.

Biiip Biiip

One year later, I did the housekeeping in a hostel.
That time, nobody told me off much.

But I got tendinitis.

The last year, I found myself in a bank. My job was
to sort account records into folders.

I was in a basement filled with cupboards,
classifying thirteen-digit numbers.

Not long after, the service was digitized,
and all the files went into the trash.

In 2005, with a brand new diploma in hand, I joined an IT services company.

These types of companies hire consultants in order to "loan them out" to other businesses as service providers for short-term missions.

With my briefcase and my new business suit, I was convinced that I had finally found my place in society.

The first few years were great. I'd wake up super motivated each morning.

Aaaah, that was a good sleep. It's sure to be a great day!

BiBiBiiiii?

I was happy to be able to say important-sounding things like ...

I've gotta go see the client tomorrow.

Ugh, I'm drowning under this workload!

I'll finish up my slides and join you in the meeting room.

My team worked well together and we were supported by our line managers.

Good job! Come on, drinks are on me.

No, seems perfect to me. I say we send it off.

I had some doubts about these results ...

But in 2009, there was a reorganization, and my branch closed.
My employer sent me on a new mission, with another colleague.

It took me an hour and a half to get to their offices.

The client wanted at least one of us to always be present.
So we had a strict work schedule which started at 8 a.m. and
finished at 8 p.m.

My colleague and I weren't allowed to eat together. Someone always had to be in the office, even during lunch break.

Of course, he didn't abide by this rule and went out to lunch with the team …

As far as the work was concerned, our instructions were always vague—when we had any.

If we asked for more details, the client seemed to get so irritated that he just made us feel stupid...

...and we didn't push the matter.
But nothing we did seemed to be right.

After a few months in that department, I'd completely lost confidence in my own ability.

My client liked to see us work late.

And he often complimented me on my appearance.

So, the more he criticized my work, the more I tried to get on his good side by working extra hours and looking elegant.

But the more I behaved this way, the more rubbish I felt. And every evening, I was anxious about going back the next day.

I started having insomnia.

The lack of sleep aggravated the situation, and after feeling incompetent for so long, I finally became incompetent.

I didn't see how I could escape my situation.
The future seemed like a dead end.

Then one morning, in the subway, my legs
refused to take me any further.

Instead of going to work, I went to see the doctor.
When I told him I had a dizzy spell, the first thing he
asked was ...

So, what are they doing
to you at work?

Um ... no, it's not them,
it's me ... sometimes I
feel faint, I ...

Ma'am, I see four cases like
yours every day. Now, what
are they putting you through
at work?

I was lucky enough to move to another company.

But that experience left its mark.

The feeling of not being good enough and drowning in the simplest tasks often overcame me.

And, even though the companies I worked for after that were less toxic, I still had the same sense of being treated like a child, of lacking freedom—of being expected to belong to my employers, body and soul.

If today's "me" told this story to the 2005 "me," back then I would have answered:

But is the solution really to look for the "good companies"?

During my career, I experienced some good work environments, where we didn't feel humiliated or held in contempt. But they weren't the majority, and crucially...at the first sign of a crisis, with the first reorganization, everything fell apart and the environment became toxic.

A typical example of this type of sea change happened when the France Télécom public utility was opened up to competition. In 2004, a reorganization plan was launched: forced mobility, work overload, and forced inactivity were all rationales used to push employees out.

A few months later, an employee stabbed himself during a meeting—and two days later, another jumped from a window.

To which Didier Lombard immediately responded with the following words:

We need to end these shocking methods of suicide!

Between 2004 and 2009, sixty of the company's employees took their own lives.

The same scenario plays out with each privatization.

For the past twenty years, employees of the French Postal Service have experienced incessant reorganization, division of labor, and unbearable increases in pace, all in the name of productivity.

In July 2016, Charles Griffond, a postman for 34 years, killed himself. He left a letter with the following explanation:

Over the last years, little by little, the Postal Service has destroyed its employees, the real postmen, those who had contact with people.

So let's move on with the Postal Service and die thanks to the Postal Service.

The unions estimate that there have been 150 suicides or attempted suicides in the Postal Service since 2007.

Same thing in the hospitals.

According to a 2015 study led by SPS, an association promoting the health of medical staff, one quarter of all nurses have already had suicidal thoughts due to their work.

I want to see an evolution in the highly rigid status of hospital employees, to develop the mobility of nursing staff.

In 2018, while the Paris University Hospital Trust was mourning the fifth suicide that year among its nursing staff, Martin Hirch, head of the Trust, declared:

At the SNCF, France's National Railway Company, unions are also raising the alarm, following one hundred suicides in three years.

We must reduce the cost of our railways.

This means thoroughly reviewing the way work is organized at the local level, focusing on adaptability ... Overall, productivity gains must increase from an average of 2.2% per year to nearly 3%.

In October 2018, a manager committed suicide at work, in Lyon. At the same time, the CEO of the SNCF, Guillaume Pepy, announced in a French newspaper:

There have been twenty new suicides since January 2019.

These examples are striking because of how the push for profits was forced upon workers over a very short time period, which rendered the measures all the more brutal.
But we're almost all familiar with the sense of unease linked to work.

Oh, no...Sunday night already...

The truth is that many of us commute to work with a knot in our stomachs.

In 2017, a French survey of over 30,000 employees showed that 52% had a high level of **anxiety**, and 29% a high level of **depression**.

If we look at this 52% in more detail, we note that women are significantly more affected than men.

57%

47%

We also see that depression increases with age and number of years worked in the company.

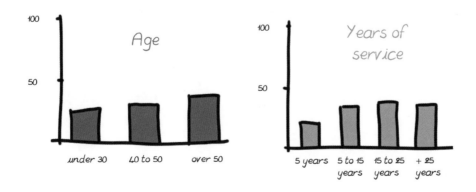

And mental distress is only part of the problem, since work also wrecks our bodies. Here are just some of the minor news items that I came across as I was writing this:

Workplace Accident at Arecelor Mittal
06/13/2019

A piece of scaffolding fell onto a worker's head

A supermarket employee lost his hand in a meat grinder

Butcher Amputated Following an Accident at Work in Vienne
06/14/2019

SUPER U Loudun

Two People in Critical Condition After an Accident at Saint-Just-Luzac
06/11/2019

A driver fell asleep at the wheel on his way to work

Daily and sometimes fatal accidents.

Workplace Accident at Lons-le-Saunier: Builder Crushed by Concrete Block
Published 06/14/2019

Lons-le-Saunier

06/14/2019
Biomass Plant Worker Dies After Being Pulled into a Machine

Employee Killed by Ride: Dramatic Accident in an Amusement Park Near Toulouse

06/14/2019

In 2017 in France, 632,918 employees suffered an injury at their place of work, and 530 died.

If we add to this the accidents that take place during commutes and work-related illnesses, we get a grand total of 766,819 injuries and 1,125 deaths.

185 168 14.5

The construction, transport, and metalworking industries account for the most employee deaths.

By comparison, the same year fifteen police officers lost their lives while out on call or on duty.

Women are not spared this fate.
    Since 2001, women have seen their risk of contracting work-related illnesses increase by 145.2%, compared to 71.5% for men.*

Cleaning personnel are particularly affected: many products contain toxic substances, like glycol, which can lead to respiratory and neurological problems, or formaldehyde, classified as a "known human carcinogen" by the IARC.**

The same is true of nail beauticians: semi-permanent nail polish, currently very fashionable, contains substances like acetaldehyde, a known carcinogen, and toluene, which is toxic for pregnant women.***

*According to Anact, the French national agency for the improvement of working conditions
**International Agency for Research on Cancer
***According to ANSES, the French Agency for Food, Environmental, and Occupational Health & Safety

We need to look at the evidence: contrary to what some people want to hammer into our brains,

I don't like the term "hardship," which suggests that work is pain. Work is emancipation, it is what gives you a place in society.

Emmanuel Macron, president of France, talking to the federation of French employers on March 28, 2017.

Work gives us the freedom to follow our dreams.

François Fillon, former prime minister of France, talking to expats in New York on September 9, 2016.

Work does not equal health.

More like illness and death.

Most studies point to the **organization of work** as the culprit behind all this suffering.

Expectations that are too high: complex tasks, not enough time, hard-to-reach objectives, etc.

Changes that are too frequent

Monday you're working on the new site down south.

At the counter, you've got three seconds to greet the customer and no more than two minutes to stamp a letter.

A lack of autonomy

Lack of support during mergers and reorganizations

Bad management

Accounts is no longer here?

Or simmering conflicts between different employees or departments.

The solution would seem to be better organization within companies.

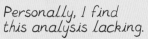

Personally, I find this analysis lacking.

It's good to want to change workplace organization, but we also need to **understand why and how** things got the way they are.

As you can imagine, it's not the result of some unfortunate circumstance.

In primitive societies, the pace of work was slow and interspersed with breaks. Each person helped produce the essential goods that were then shared out among everyone.

The people of the Yanomami tribe in the Amazon worked on average forty hours per week, domestic tasks included.

The concepts of **profit** and **private property** were nonexistent.

Ten thousand years ago, thanks to agriculture and livestock farming, populations became more sedentary. It became possible to produce enough to live on without the participation of the whole community.

Better productivity led to a food surplus, which could be **stored** and **exchanged**.

Freed from the need to work to produce "essential goods," certain communities could focus on other tasks, like crafts.

The cattle, the buildings, and then the land went from being **collective to being privately owned**. Society split into different groups, each with its own area of expertise, and its own interests.

Quite quickly, certain groups like the village chieftains, soldiers, or priests organized themselves to take over a large share of the property.

Society split up into **different classes**.

Under the feudal system, from the ninth to the thirteenth centuries, there were essentially two classes: the nobility and the serfs.

The nobility owned the land and the serfs had to pay for its "use" in money or kind.

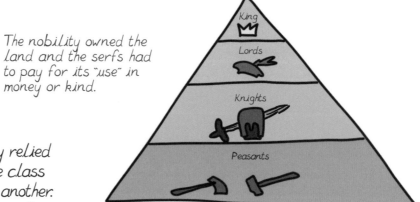

This system already relied on the labor of one class being exploited by another.
    But the serfs were "free" to decide how and at what pace they labored the earth.

182

Toward the end of the Middle Ages, the feudal system was turned on its head thanks to global navigation by sea.

Some families could start to accumulate capital in the form of gold, growing rich off the back of slaves and colonial trade.

Here you store the gold, sell the American produce, and load ships with European merchandise.

Here you exchange slaves for American produce: coffee, cotton, gold, etc.

Here you exchange European merchandise for slaves.

A new class emerged: **the merchant bourgeoisie.**

The bourgeoisie discovered and coveted new markets. But feudal production methods limited its expansion.

My lord, do you not see that this peasant is idling? His child is playing instead of digging!

What's it to me? As long as they pay me their tithe...

Well, you could increase the crop yield and sell the surplus!

Little by little, the feudal system lost its foothold to the bourgeoisie.

With the gold they amassed by pillaging new territories, members of the bourgeoisie created the first factories. This meant they could optimize production and maximize profits. **The time spent working** became an important factor.

Hey! Enough hanging around!

The belfry clock was used to control workers (but they also attempted to seize it and fight back by sounding a call to revolt!)

In France, the bourgeoisie finally took over with the revolution of 1789.

After eradicating the feudal power structure, members of the bourgeoisie set up more and more factories ... **but never worked in them!**

The merchandise was produced by the **working** class in exchange for a salary, and **remained the property of the bourgeoisie,** who sold it to make profits.

Thanks for helping out! Now the king's out of the way, the right to private property is written into the law, and everyone can access it!

Sure, but ...what do we do if we're penniless?

Ah, bad luck ...but you can come work in my factory!

With the rural exodus, the abundant workforce was pushed toward the cities by famine. This allowed factory owners to impose whatever working conditions they wanted on their employees.

You work 12 hours a day for 40 cents an hour. If it doesn't suit you, move out of the way, others are waiting.

Not tired

Tired, but who cares

And technological progress, notably the invention of the steam engine, meant that production could be uninterrupted, no longer adjusting to daylight hours or weather conditions.

It's the start of an era in which **humans have to adapt to machines and profit goals.**

In the early twentieth century, new forms of work organization emerged. Taylorism, and then Fordism, sought to extract the expertise from the brains of workers, and split it up into simple and repetitive tasks.

Vertical split between design and creation

And horizontal split between the different stages of one process

This meant their skills were no longer needed, so they were replaceable, and the balance of power swung toward employers.

This was also the idea behind western imperial policies: create an unequal power relationship in order to better exploit foreign laborers.

That was the case with slavery.

And still today, when migrants are captured at sea and exploited on fishing boats, only to be thrown back into the water once they're too sick to work.

Or in Indian sugarcane plantations, where female workers are forced to have their uteruses removed so that their periods don't disrupt productivity.

Over the years, our ancestors were able to organize and install a few safeguards to protect themselves...

Labor Inspection in 1892

This child has worked more than the authorized hours!

Social Security in 1945

The state of your lungs means you can no longer work, but you'll still be covered.

This report describes the impact of voice commands on our mental health.

The Health and Safety Committee in 1982

But the bourgeoisie and, by extension, our governments are consciously dismantling this progress, piece by piece.

In 2016, a labor law replaced medical visits with "informational" visits.

In 2014, after the retirement age was increased, a hardship account was set up ... and then abolished in 2017.

In 2018, health and safety committees, works councils, and staff representatives were all merged into a single entity, which has to manage the three tasks with fewer people and means.

It's not that there isn't resistance, but the power balance is very uneven. Although in the minority, the bourgeoisie can defend its interests with very effective weapons.

Like <u>morality,</u>

Remember that time is money. He that can earn ten shillings a day by his labor, and goes abroad, or sits idle one half of that day, tho' he spends but sixpence during his diversion or idleness, ought not to reckon that the only expence: he has really spent or rather thrown away five shillings besides.

Benjamin Franklin, in "Advice to a Young Tradesman" (1748)

<u>religion,</u>

God has already decided whether you shall go to heaven or hell.

Ah. Might as well rest then.

Well, know that only those chosen for heaven succeed in their search for riches. If you succeed, then you have been chosen.

How convenient

the threat of unemployment and poverty,

Who's willing to work Sundays? It's optional, of course.

Just remember that you're still in your trial period...

and, if necessary, force.

In France, in 1948, miners went on a massive strike to denounce decrees that eliminated guaranteed wages, among other things. Jules Moch, then interior minister, first pretended to engage in a dialogue in order to "ensure the safety and freedom of work." Then, once this failed, he ordered the riot police to open fire on the strikers. One hundred miners died.

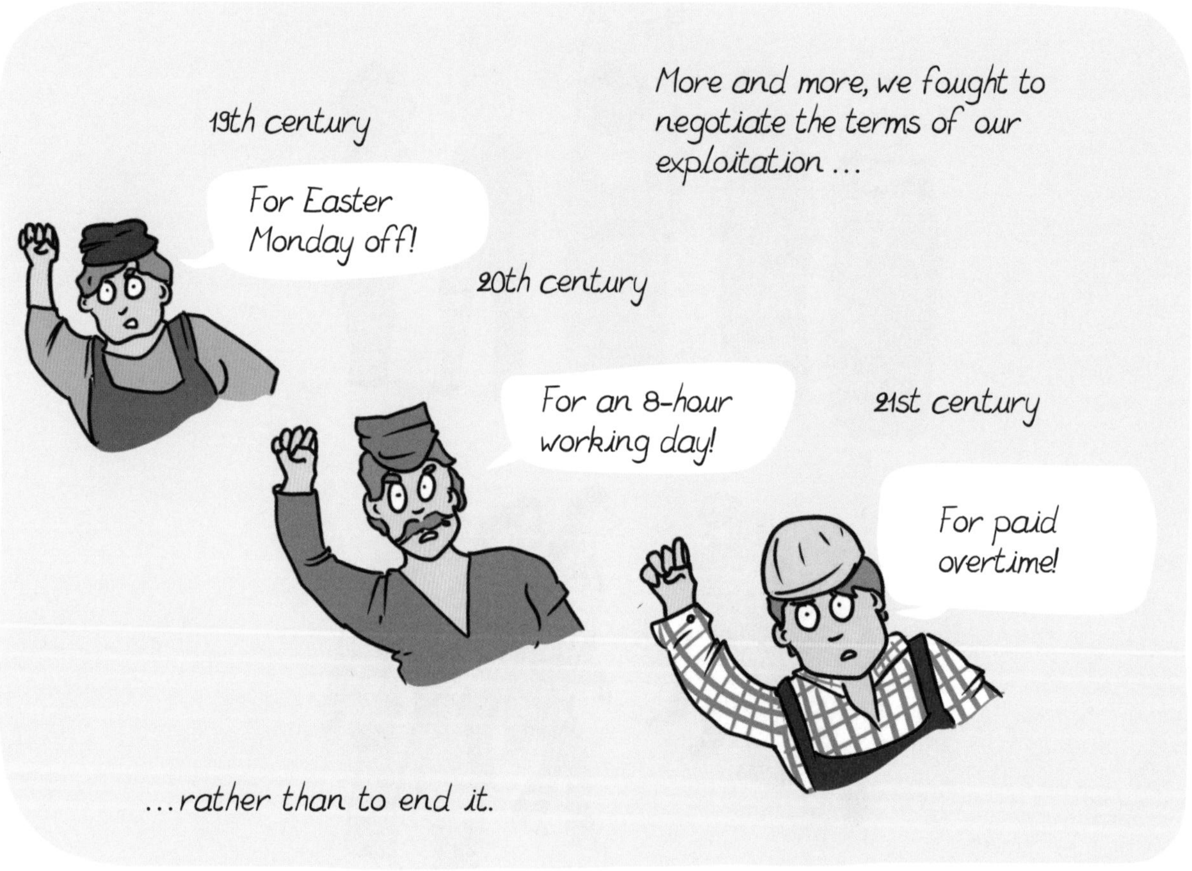
More and more, we fought to negotiate the terms of our exploitation ...
19th century
For Easter Monday off!
20th century
For an 8-hour working day!
21st century
For paid overtime!
...rather than to end it.

Yet that's exactly what we need to do: refuse to be exploited, not negotiate the details!

Because for as long as we are in this power relationship, however significant our victories, they will only be a patch on an unfair situation.

The bourgeoisie will keep doing all they can to undo the achievements that our predecessors fought for. They'll use each new crisis to remove some of our safety nets—and we'll have to start again from scratch.

The only long-term solution is to take away their power. And we've got plenty of it ourselves, since without us, they're nothing!

Employers aren't the ones producing . . . we are!

So, they didn't buy our talk of social dialogue. Shall we send in the riot police?

Afraid not, George. The police are saying they're not paid enough to face that.

THE BOSS NEEDS YOU, YOU DON'T NEED HIM!

GENERAL STRIKE

Our power lies there: in our class consciousness.

I'd really like to tell all this to the 2009 "me," who felt so insignificant after being shuffled from one job to another, like a machine.

Hey, you're the one doing the work!

Your boss needs you more than the other way around . . .

192

But I doubt I would have been ready to hear it.

What do you mean, I don't need him? No job—no wages!

Yes...but if you guys don't work, then no wages for him either.

He's not giving you work out of kindness, but because he earns money from your labor.

But still, starting this business was his idea, he had a good **marketing strategy** and he took risks!

Risks? Well, first we need to be clear what risks we're talking about...Dying on a construction site? Or on the road? Or having a burn-out? No, the only thing he risks is potentially losing his fortune. And in that case...he becomes like us!

And we're not talking about small, local businesses, but big companies that are listed on the stock exchange. So even this "risk" of sacrificing their luxurious lives, of having to live like the rest of us, do you image these CEOs are facing it? Let's look at who we're dealing with.

Behind these large companies, we often find the heirs of bourgeois families from previous centuries.

Let's consider, for example, a certain Wendel family.

They created their fortune in the 18th century by purchasing foundries to provide a military arsenal for the monarchy. Thousands of miners lost their lives for the sake of this dynasty.

The Wendels were nobles. They were chased away during the French Revolution.

That was a close one, Françoise!

Indeed, François, indeed!

They came back twenty years later and bought back their foundries with the help of a certain Seillière.

Do you not think, colonel, that the people need a strong State?

Their exile had taught them a lesson, and the family became very involved in repressing the labor movement. Together with the Rothschilds, the descendants of François de Wendel financed a nationalist party, the PSF.*

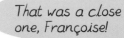

Indeed, Mr. Wendel, indeed.

*The Parti Social Français (French Social Party) was founded in 1936 by Colonel François de la Rocque. It was a right-wing conservative and nationalist party.

Their successors benefited from the war, and expanded their empire during the twentieth century. In 1970, their foundries produced three-quarters of all French steel.

Hey there!

Hi, plebs!

Among the heirs to this fortune we find a certain Ernest-Antoine Seillière and Françoise de Panafieu.

But the economic crisis threatened the steel industry. The heirs handed over the foundries to the State and left with the capital. Hundreds of thousands of workers became unemployed.

Right then, have fun with the lay-offs!

The family's successors reinvested the billions handed over by the State into profitable businesses: car suppliers, a chain of opticians, and ... look at that, an IT services company.

Oh.

Since then, the group has thrived by investing and divesting its capital here and there. Yet its directors have been accused of fiscal fraud—an investigation that has dragged on for ten years with no end in sight.

So those are the risks. Now, let's talk about that **strategy** you mentioned. In reality, employees are the ones most likely to come up with good ideas. After all, they know the job! It's just that no one asks for their opinion ... And to some extent, if you need a strategy to sell something, then maybe that thing isn't really something that's needed.

If we abandoned this market logic, and if companies belonged to everyone, we wouldn't need strategies! Either the products are useful, and we make them, or they're not, and we close shop or make something else.

Another thing: unemployment. Today, it's super useful for employers, who use it to dictate their own rules, since everyone's looking for work ...

The 2-Hour Workday, a book published in 1977 by the Adret collective, explains how it would be possible to drastically reduce our working hours while maintaining the same standard of living: manufacturing less, sharing more, improving sustainability, dividing up work better, etc.

But if we're the ones running the show, we can share the work among everyone, so that we all work, but less.

In fact, we could all live well and only need to work two hours a day.

196

That all seems like a utopia to me.

It seems like a utopia because our imaginations are constrained, starting in childhood. We're conditioned to think that society can't change, or maybe just on the fringes.

Work, consume, have kids, vote, and above all, keep quiet.

But to build something, we have to imagine it first. Come on, let's give it a go.

Instead of adapting workers to machines, we'd do the opposite. Technology would relieve us of the most arduous tasks.

To start off, we need to leave the profit logic behind. The means of production would be owned by the community, not private individuals.

Then, since we'd be working for the good of society, and not for a salary, we would separate the necessary from the superfluous.

We could finally be glad that some of our jobs are disappearing!

We might also imagine schools that aren't there to mold us into docile workers. Children would no longer be forced to sit in one place for hours on end. They'd be free to move, share their opinions, and choose their subjects.

Great, welcome to La-La Land. It's never gonna happen. If people aren't forced to work, they'll just become lazy. It's human nature.

Aaaah, human nature! Another old myth. There's no such thing as human nature. We reflect an image of our society. Today, for sure, it's individualistic.

But in a communist world, since that's what I'm describing, work exists to be useful to everyone. So we'd have good reason to participate. The idea is that when a community is there to help us out, then we're also willing to help the community. It's a kind of virtuous circle.

And is laziness really a vice?

In a class-based society, the dominant group imposes morals that serve its interests. So today, being idle is bad because we need worker-machines. But maybe tomorrow, taking the time to read and daydream will be a positive thing.

OK, I get it. But then, how do we make it happen? It seems like an impossible dream.

Sure. That's where it gets complicated. As you can imagine, the bourgeoisie isn't going to let its precious factories be collectivized just like that.

But remember what I said: all the wealth comes from **our** labor. We're the ones with the power! If we go on strike, we block everything. The problem is that people haven't realized this yet. For things to change, we need to develop our **class consciousness** and revolt **en masse**.

Then, the community as a whole could get back what belongs to everyone. And the bourgeoisie would go to work, two hours a day, like everyone else. I'm sure they'd survive.

But there's lots more you still have to experience before you develop a class consciousness.

So have a safe trip, and you'll see, you're not alone!

Emma.

9

Just Being Nice

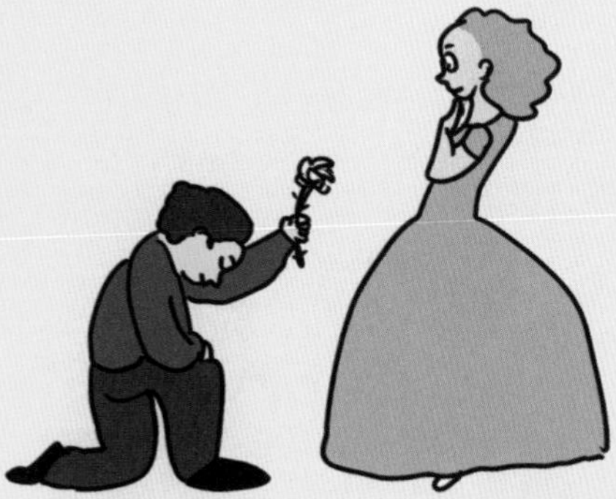

When I started working in IT, I was surprised to often get the same question.

It's not too tough working with guys?

Well ... no, it's great!

At that time, my gender seemed to be an advantage.

All good with the code? If you need any help, just give me a shout.

Aw, thanks, that's kind of you. I'm fine for now, I'll let you know if I get stuck!

I could see my managers were more eager to help me than my male coworkers, but that seemed like a positive thing.

A few years later, I wanted to take on more responsibilities.

> I'm very familiar with the project and the client, and since our manager's leaving, I'd like to replace him.

> Hmm, I think it's a bit early for you. We have someone with a little more experience in mind.

It wasn't looking likely, so I quit that job to become a manager at another company.

But my new position only met my expectations on paper: I had no responsibilities at all.

> We really need someone with your interpersonal skills, you're gonna be a lifesaver.

> You won't be managing your own team, but you'll set everyone's schedules and check that the developers are on track.

It still seemed like a good job, so I accepted.

My workday involved visiting the developers and employing my "interpersonal skills" to make sure that they were sticking to their schedule.

But it didn't work all that well.

After a year, I had a performance review with my manager.

We're so happy to have you here, you're so nice and positive, your presence really brightens up the place!

Nothing but compliments. So why did I feel so disparaged?

Level of self-esteem: 0

I needed someone else's perspective to finally get it.

So, did the review go well?

Em...not bad, I got a great evaluation and nice comments.

But, I don't know ...I don't feel satisfied. Take a look.

"Brightens up the place"??? What does he take you for, a plant? There's nothing here about your work.

Did you smash his teeth in when he said this to you?

My hairy man's legendary finesse

There you go, it's all about my attitude. As if all the work I did was pointless.

And a few days later, during a conversation with a feminist friend of mine, I realized what I was up against.

Everything still sunny in that man's world of yours?

Pfff. They're perfectly nice, always giving me compliments ... but what I'd really like is for them to comment on my work, not the color of my dresses. I know they're just being friendly, but I'm feeling like an ornament.

Girl, no, they're not just being nice. What you're saying screams **benevolent sexism** to me.

Huh?

Benevolent sexism is all about treating women like fragile little creatures that must be protected.

Two psychologists, Susan Fiske and Peter Glick, developed this concept in 1996 during their research.

It means that while women are being placed on a pedestal and lauded for their supposedly feminine qualities ...

...they're being thought of as incompetent in other areas.

Contrary to hostile sexism, which is easy to identify...

Oh, sorry, no, we're looking for a man. Otherwise there's too much drama...

But that's illegal!

...benevolent sexism often comes across as well-meaning.

Ah, it'll be nice to have a feminine vibe in the office, it'll improve communication, we're a bit useless at that, ha ha!

Em...OK, just as well then...

So its victims rarely identify it as such.

The most common way it's expressed is well known: gallantry.

After you, miss.

Because we women are incapable of opening doors ourselves ...

As opposed to politeness, which is indifferent to gender, gallantry is defined as "courteous attention toward women."

Today, this practice still plays a big part in heterosexual seduction.

I'm paying because I'm interested in her.

He's paying, so he must consider my company worthwhile.

Yet it implies a rather unequal exchange of services.

Another frequent expression of benevolent sexism is the "women-are-wonderful effect."

Highlighted in 1994 by two psychologists, Alice Eagly and Antonio Mladinic, the women-are-wonderful effect consists in over-estimating—culturally but not financially—traditional feminine attributes: gentleness, sensitivity, delicacy, etc.

This ad campaign called "Thank you, Mom," for a big brand of cleaning products, praises mothers who sacrifice themselves for their children's sporting careers.

It's true that at first glance, this form of sexism might seem inoffensive, even beneficial.

Personally, I like getting flowers and having my bag carried. It's nice!

And at work, as soon as I need help, some-one jumps right in—it's rather useful!

But this benevolence is only present on the surface, when there's little at stake.
    When things get heated, it tends to evaporate.

For example, let's look at the "women-and-children-first principle," which in our collective imagination applies in case of shipwreck. On the *Titanic*, this is indeed what happened...

...but it's hardly a general rule. In reality, it's more like ...the privileged first!

When the *Titanic* sank, 70% of women survived compared to only 20% of men—but it must be added that the ship's captain ordered that anyone who did not respect the rule was to be shot.

In 2012, two Swedish researchers, Mikael Elinder and Oscar Erixson, studied the data from eighteen shipwrecks that took place over the last three centuries. Their conclusions are unequivocal: those with the highest rate of survival are ...the crew!
    And those with the lowest rate are children.

61%

37%

27%

15%

For the authors of this study,
the outcome is logical, since:

Rational individuals,
whether they're egotisti-
cal or empathetic, make
a cost-benefit analysis
before helping others.

Giving a compliment, offering flowers, holding a door, that
all has a good cost-benefit ratio.
   But when it comes to saving your own skin—not so much!

Gallant gestures come at a low cost...for men!
   Whereas for women, they have a price: being trapped in a position of
dependence, in the role of a princess waiting to be saved.

I could just cut my hair and
use it as a rope, but I think
I'd rather wait for a real
man to come and save me!

And they influence the extent to which we feel competent...

In 2006, psychologists Marie Lar-chet and Benoît Dardenne did an experiment: they ran simulations of job interviews, followed by a memory test. During the interviews, the recruiter slipped in different comments to different groups:

We're looking for a man or woman with a profile that matches yours.

Neutral,

Women don't think logically.

Women need to be protected by men.

On the memory test, the group faced with be-nevolent sexism did worse than the other two groups.

showing hostile sexism,   or benevolent sexism.

...and the day we want to leave our gilded cage, the backlash is harsh.

As shown by the avalanche of comments on Twitter when a feminist author, Valérie Rey-Robert, set out to question the idea of gallantry.

 @superGalant

An advance warning: the first cranky chick who gets her panties in a twist 'cause I hold a door open for her is likely to get a kick up the backside, and that's just to teach her some basic manners.

 @princeSuperCharming

Where I come from, it's impolite not to hold open a door. But feel free to refuse, and I'll happily slam it back in your snout.

According to Fiske and Glick, sexism therefore has two sides:

one hostile and well-recognized, which consists in denying women access to areas deemed "important,"

and the other falsely benevolent, which consists in praising their skills in traditionally feminine and undervalued tasks.

The stick

The carrot

These two sides combined are what they term **ambivalent sexism.**

According to their research, this ambivalence stems from the cohabitation of two types of power:

structural power, which places men in dominant positions by way of politics, law, media, and religion,

and dyadic power, which makes men dependent on women for sex and reproduction.

Witch!

Princess...

So hostile and benevolent sexism are not mutually exclusive...

With, on the one hand, those who dislike women,

and, on the other, those who venerate them.

Women are devious and manipulative!

No! They're gentle and beautiful!

...on the contrary, these two types of sexism complement each other.

I loooove women! They're so gentle, so pure...so much more sensitive than us men.

Well, the respect-able ones at least. 'Cause the ones in mini-skirts who'll sleep with anyone and everyone...they could do with having some sense slapped into them!

It's the two components brought together, the carrot and the stick, that keep us in our subordinate positions.

I experienced this at work, when, once I realized that I was being subjected to a form of sexism, I stopped trying to fit the mold that I'd been assigned.

BEFORE

Hey, please don't forget the corrections this evening, you left early yesterday so we weren't able to send them in ...thanks!

We still need those corrections, I'll leave you to finish and send them in yourself.

AFTER

The backlash was quick to come.

Your attitude has changed these past few months. I find you've become, how should I put it ...arrogant.

I've decided to change things around a bit.

I was demoted.

We're also very familiar with the flip side of the "compliments" we get in the street.

Hey, I just complimented you, you could at least answer!

I'm talking to you, bitch!

Pfff, you're freakin' ugly anyway.

And the treatment reserved for women who "interfere" in politics.

In 2013, a French deputy, Philippe Le Ray, stood out by clucking at the Green Party's Véronique Massonneau, distracting her from her speech.

Bak, bak, bak, baaaaak!

Stop that!

And in 2017, the goat-like cries made by an unidentified deputy disrupted another female politician, Alice Thourot.

Certain parliamentary committees will be looking into this ...into this topic ...as for me ...um ...as for myself ...

Baaaaaah-baaah baah

218

So there you have it, once I saw things though this lens, many events in my work life took on a whole new meaning!

The flowers I got on March 8, the bosses complimenting my smile ... it all seemed suddenly like more bars on the cage I had to escape from, now more than ever.

So I stopped conforming to patriarchal conventions. I started refusing tasks that weren't related to my position but were given to me because of my gender, like organizing events or welcoming visitors.

But I paid a high price, since I was demoted. I realized that setting out to change all this by myself would mean embarking on a path through a battleground.

And that I needed to talk about these things with others, so that together we could make a difference.

In France, men shake hands with male colleagues and kiss female colleagues on the cheek, but women are expected to kiss everyone! But my female colleagues and I realized that we didn't much like having to go around kissing everyone on the cheek, just because we were women.

So, one morning, we coordinated to change this custom: we simply shook hands with everyone, and that was that.

It worked because there were a number of us, and that gave us courage and a feeling of legitimacy.

Of course, it was just a small victory, but each victory, however small, leads to the next, and that's how we move forward.

By sticking together when we need to, by systematically denouncing every instance of sexism in the public sphere, and by discussing it, including exposing what lies behind the mask of false benevolence ...

So that one day, we can finally be free of gender roles and everything else that's been assigned to us!

Emma.

Bibliography

It's Not Right, But . . .

"Comment lutter contre le viol," Crêpe Georgette blog

"De la banalité des violences sexuelles," Crêpe Georgette blog

"Les hommes sont-ils tous des violeurs?," Crêpe Georgette blog

"Et des porcs furent balancés," Usul, *Ouvrez les guillemets* YouTube channel

"Tea Consent" (video)

A Role to Play

"J'ai mis des petits lapins," Crocodiles Project blog (comic strip)

"Paye Ta Schneck," on the difference between flirting and harassment (tutorial)

"Harcèlement de rue ou compliment? Je veux comprendre," madmoiZelle webzine

The Story of a Guardian of the Peace

Journal d'un gardien de la paix, Erik Blondin, La Fabrique Editions, 2002

"Dans la police" radio episode, *Les Pieds sur Scène* radio show, France Culture

Michelle

"Les variations de niveau de vie des hommes et des femmes à la suite d'un divorce ou d'une rupture de Pacs," Carole Bonnet, Bertrand Garbinti and Anne Solaz, INSEE (French Institute of Statistics), 2015

"Les écarts de pension entre les femmes et les hommes: un état des lieux en Europe," Marco Geraci and Anne Lavigne, INSEE (French Institute of Statistics), 2017

"Les retraites des femmes nettement inférieures à celles des hommes,"—Erwan Auger, Thomas Ducharne and Sophie Villaume, INSEE (French Institute of Statistics), 2017

The Conflict: Woman & Mother, Élisabeth Badinter, Text Publishing, 2012

"Les fondements politico-économiques du fémonationalisme," *Sara Farris, Contretemps website*

"Au nom des droits des femmes? Fémonationalisme et néolibéralisme,"*Sara Farris, Contretemps website*

In the Name of Women's Rights: the Rise of Femonationalism, Sara Farris, Duke University Press Books, 2017

Caliban and the Witch, Silvia Federici, Autonomedia, 2004

Women, Race and Class, Angela Y. Davis, Vintage Books, 1983

"Le 'travail ménager,' son 'partage inégal' et comment le combattre," Christine Delphy, Les Mots Sont Importants website

The Main Enemy: A Materialist Analysis of Women's Oppression, Christine Delphy, Women's Research and Resources Centre Publications, 1977

The Power of Love

"Emotional Labor Around the World: An Interview with Arlie Hochschild," Global Dialogue website

The Managed Heart: Commercialization of Human Feeling, Arlie Russell Hochschild, University of California Press, 2012

"Les Françaises et l'orgasme," IFOP (French Public Opinion Institute), 2015

Love Power and Political Interests: Towards a Theory of Patriarchy in Contemporary Western

Societies, Anna G. Jónasdóttir, University of Örebro, 1991

Why Women Are Oppressed, Anna G. Jónasdóttir, Temple University Press, 1994

Les sentiments du prince Charles, Liv Strömquist, Reservoir Books, 2019

"Sexual Functioning Among Young Adult Cancer Patients: A 2-year Longitudinal Study," Chiara Acquati et al., *Cancer* journal

"Le veuvage et après," Christine Guilbault, CAIRN website

"Why Women Are Tired: The Price of Unpaid Emotional Labor," Christine Hutchison, Huffington Post website

"'Women Are Just Better at This Stuff': Is Emotional Labor Feminism's Next Frontier?," Rose Hackman, Guardian website

"'Where's My Cut?': On Unpaid Emotional Labor," Jess Zimmerman, Toast website

"L'impuissance comme idéal de beauté des femmes—le sourire," Noémie Renard, Antisexisme website

Consequences

"Harcèlement sexuel et sexiste dans les transports: résultats d'une étude menée à Bordeaux," French High Council for Gender Equality

"Contraception et IVG," INSEE (French Institute of Statistics)

"Quelles sont les méthodes de contraception les plus utilisées dans le monde?" INED (French Institute for Demographic Studies)

It's All in Your Head

"Les luttes pour le salaire ménager: théorie et pratique," Contretemps website

"La vie quotidienne en France depuis 1974. Les enseignements de l'enquête Emploi du temps," INSEE (French Institute of Statistics)

"En 25 ans, moins de tâches domestiques pour les femmes, l'écart de situation avec les hommes se réduit," INSEE (French Institute of Statistics)

"La gestion ordinaire de la vie en deux," Monique Haicault, Sociologie du Travail, 1984

"Travail parental et charge mentale," En aparté website

"Espagne: une grève générale féministe sans précédent mobilise 5 millions de personnes," Les Inrocks website

"En Espagne, le congé de paternité passe de 5 à 8 semaines,"—Le Monde website

"Le premier ministre Édouard Philippe face à la rédaction," Mediapart website

"'Je ne veux pas d'une société de la délation,' affirme Emmanuel Macron," BMFTV (video)

Une culture du viol à la française, Valérie Rey-Robert, Libertalia, 2019

Sunday Evenings

"Didier Lombard aux salariés d'Orange: 'La pêche aux moules, c'est fini,'" Mediapart website

"Un salarié de France Télécom se poignarde en pleine réunion," Le Figaro website

"Une employée de France Télécom se défenestre et décède," 20Minutes website

"Suicides à France Télécom: le rappel des faits," Le Figaro website

"Vague de suicides alarmante à La Poste," Le Figaro website

"Suicide et professionnels de santé: le poids des chiffres," Site Infirmiers website

"Mediapart - AP-HP: en dépit des alertes multiples, Hirsch veut tenir le cap de l'austérité," NPA2009 website

"Suicides et travail: la SNCF sur la voie de France Télécom," NPA2009 website

"Observatoire de la sante psychologique au travail evaluation du stress," Stimulus (report)

"Grande-Synthe Accident du travail chez ArcelorMittal, un homme de 52 ans entre la vie et la mort," La Voix du Nord website

"Vienne: un boucher amputé après un accident du travail," Forum website

"Deux personnes grièvement blessées dans accident à Saint-Just-Luzac," France Bleu website

"Accident du travail à Lons-le-Saunier: un bloc de béton écrase un ouvrier," France Info website

"Happé par une machine, l'employé d'une centrale de biomasse décède à Brignoles," Var Matin website

"Dramatique accident dans un parc d'attraction, près de Toulouse: un employé tué par un manège," Actu Toulouse website

Twitter account @DuAccident: "Accident du travail: silence des ouvriers meurent"

"Risque accident du travail: Statistiques sur la sinistralité de l'année 2017 suivant la nomenclature d'activités française (NAF)," Ameli (study)

"Photographie statistique des accidents de travail, des accidents de trajet et des maladies professionnelles en France selon le sexe entre 2001 et 2016," ANACT (study)

"Les travailleurs des ongleries en danger," L'Express website

"Macron veut supprimer le nom du compte pénibilité," BMFTV (study)

"François Fillon: 'il serait temps que les Français acceptent la précarité,'"

Mediapart website

"Propriété privée," Wikirouge website

"Surpêche - la fin du poisson à foison," ARTE

"Inde: des travailleuses des champs privées de leur utérus 'pour améliorer leur rendement,'" RTBF website

"Permis de tuer: Enquête sur la lutte du grand patronat contre la santé au travail," Frustration webzine

"Les vies brisées des mineurs grévistes de 1948 au grand jour," Libération website

"Sidérurgie lorraine - Des de Wendel à Mittal: l'enrichissement ininterrompu des grandes familles bourgeoises," Lutte Ouvrière website

Travailler deux heures par jour, Adret Collective, 1977

Just Being Nice

"Le sexisme bienveillant comme processus de maintien des inégalités sociales entre les genres," Marie Sarlet and Benoit Dardenne, CAIRN website

"La galanterie est une forme de sexisme," Crêpe Georgette blog

"Women Are Wonderful Effect," Wikipedia

"Every Man for Himself! Gender, Norms and Survival in Maritime Disasters," Mikael Elinder and Oscar Erixson, Research Institute of Industrial Economics

"À l'Assemblée nationale: 'Arrêtez, je ne suis pas une poule!,'" Le Monde website

"'Cris de chèvre' à l'Assemblée: François de Rugy assure que 'l'auteur sera sanctionné,'" Europe1 website